ABRAHAM LINCOLN
TO PRESERVE THE UNION

THE HISTORY OF THE CIVIL WAR

THE HISTORY OF THE CIVIL WAR

ABRAHAM LINCOLN

TO PRESERVE THE UNION

by RUSSELL SHORTO

INTRODUCTORY ESSAY BY

HENRY STEELE COMMAGER

SILVER BURDETT PRESS

Series Editorial Supervisor: Richard G. Gallin
Series Editing: Agincourt Press
Series Consultant: Elizabeth Fortson
Cover and Text Design: Circa 86, New York
Series Supervision of Art and Design: Leslie Bauman
Maps: Susan Johnston Carlson

Consultants: Richard M. Haynes, Assistant Professor, Division of
Administration, Curriculum, and Instruction, Western Carolina
University; Karen E. Markoe, Professor of History, Maritime
College of the State University of New York.

Library of Congress Cataloging-in-Publication Data
Shorto, Russell.
    Abraham Lincoln : to preserve the union / by Russell Shorto.
        p.   cm. — (The History of the Civil War)
    Includes bibliograpical references (p.   ).
    Summary: A biography of the President who led the country through
the stormy years of the Civil War.
    1. Lincoln, Abraham, 1809-1865—Juvenile literature.
    2. Presidents—United States—Biography—Juvenile literature.
    3. United States—History—Civil War, 1861-1865—Juvenile
literature. [1. Lincoln, Abraham, 1809-1865.   2. Presidents.]
    I. Title. II. Series.
    E457.905.S48   1990
    973.7'092—dc20
    [B]
    [92]   90-32367
    ISBN 0-382-09937-0 (lib. bdg.)   ISBN 0-382-24046-4 (pbk.)   CIP
                                                                          AC

TABLE OF CONTENTS

Abraham Lincoln was born on a hard-scrabble farm in frontier Kentucky—"born," as he himself put it, "in the most humble walks of life." His mother, whom he loved dearly, died when he was a boy of nine. His father remarried, and in time little Abe came to love his stepmother. Abe went to country schools—first in Kentucky and then, when the family moved across the Ohio River, in Indiana—where he got a smattering of education and discovered the treasure-house of knowledge in books.

In 1830, when he was 21 years old, he moved west to the little town of New Salem, Illinois. Here he took a miscellany of jobs: clerking in a country store, acting as local postmaster, and serving as a captain in the Black Hawk War between Illinois settlers and the Sauk-Fox Indian nation. (Lincoln saw no action against Indians in the war but, he later said, took part in "a good many bloody struggles with the mosquitoes.")

But what really attracted him was the law. Somehow he acquired a few law books, which he studied in his spare time. In 1837, he moved to Springfield, the new capital of Illinois. There he was admitted to the bar and set up shop as an attorney. His long-time partner, William Herndon, considered him a brilliant lawyer but careless about the little details of life. As often as not, he used his silk stovepipe hat as a briefcase, filing letters, notes, and his bank book in it.

Over the next few years, Abe Lincoln followed the court on its circuit from one country seat to another. The towns were small and the cases usually were as well. But they provided Lincoln with invaluable training. For while it may have been Lincoln the prairie politician who ultimately rose to the highest office in the land, it was Lincoln the lawyer who successfully prosecuted the War Between the States, and who argued the case for emancipation of the slaves. In those two "cases," his clients were the United States of America and the four million black Americans who had lived all their lives in slavery. It is because he won both of those cases that he has become the most beloved of all American presidents.

That claim is not hard to support. George Washington, to be sure, was the great creator of the Union. Without him, it is uncertain whether the weak alliance of states that won the Revolutionary War would have been able to transform itself into the strong federation that grew and prospered over the following decades. But the federation finally split apart in 1861, and it was Abraham Lincoln who led the nation through its greatest crisis and preserved the Union.

Beyond that, Lincoln was able to do something that no one else in modern history has ever done. He gave four million men, women, and children a chance at a new and happier life, and ensured it for their descendants for generations to come, by putting an end to slavery. If Washington is the symbol of the creation of the Union, Lincoln became the Great Emancipator. Both were commanders–in–chief who led their armies to victories that changed the history of mankind.

CIVIL WAR TIME LINE

May 22
Kansas-Nebraska Act states that in new territories the question of slavery will be decided by the citizens. Many Northerners are outraged because this act could lead to the extension of slavery.

1854	1855	1856	1857

May 21
Lawrence, Kansas is sacked by proslavery Missourians.
May 22
Senator Charles Sumner is caned by Preston Brooks for delivering a speech against slavery.
May 24 – 25
Pottawatomie Creek massacre committed by John Brown and four of his sons.

March 6
The Supreme Court, in the *Dred Scott* ruling, declares that blacks are not U. S. citizens, and therefore cannot bring lawsuits. The ruling divides the country on the question of the legal status of blacks.

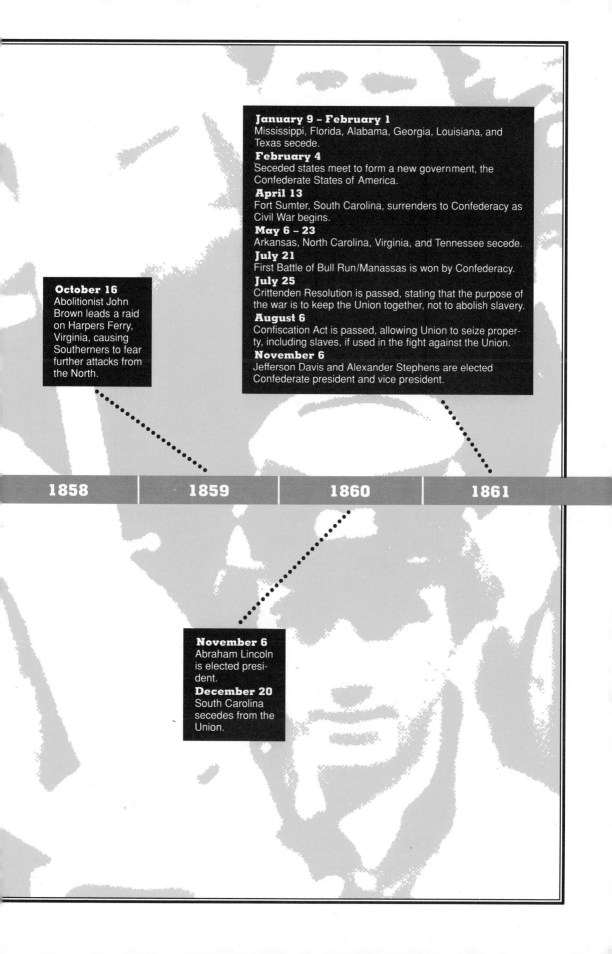

October 16
Abolitionist John Brown leads a raid on Harpers Ferry, Virginia, causing Southerners to fear further attacks from the North.

January 9 – February 1
Mississippi, Florida, Alabama, Georgia, Louisiana, and Texas secede.
February 4
Seceded states meet to form a new government, the Confederate States of America.
April 13
Fort Sumter, South Carolina, surrenders to Confederacy as Civil War begins.
May 6 – 23
Arkansas, North Carolina, Virginia, and Tennessee secede.
July 21
First Battle of Bull Run/Manassas is won by Confederacy.
July 25
Crittenden Resolution is passed, stating that the purpose of the war is to keep the Union together, not to abolish slavery.
August 6
Confiscation Act is passed, allowing Union to seize property, including slaves, if used in the fight against the Union.
November 6
Jefferson Davis and Alexander Stephens are elected Confederate president and vice president.

1858 | **1859** | **1860** | **1861**

November 6
Abraham Lincoln is elected president.
December 20
South Carolina secedes from the Union.

February 6
Fort Henry, Tennessee, is captured.
February 16
Fort Donelson, Tennessee, is captured by Union.
March 9
Monitor and *Merrimack* battle near Hampton Roads, Virginia.
March 23
Shenandoah Valley Campaign opens with Union victory over Maj. Gen. Thomas J. "Stonewall" Jackson.
April 7
Gen. Ulysses S. Grant wins Battle of Shiloh, Tennessee, splitting rebel forces on the Mississippi River.
April 25
New Orleans is captured by Union naval forces led by flag officer David Farragut.
June 19
Slavery is abolished in U. S. territories.
June 25
Gen. Robert E. Lee leads rout of Gen. George McClellan's army in the Seven Days Battles.
July 17
The United States Congress authorizes formation of the first black regiments.
August 29 – 30
Second Battle of Bull Run/Manassas is won by Confederacy.
September 5
Lee leads first Confederate invasion of the North into Maryland.
September 17
Battle of Antietam/Sharpsburg, bloodiest of the war, ends in a stalemate between Lee and McClellan.

1862	1863	1864	1865

January 1
Lincoln issues Emancipation Proclamation, freeing slaves in Confederate states.
March 3
U.S. Congress passes its first military draft.
April 2
Bread riots occur in Richmond, Virginia.
May 1 – 4
Battle of Chancellorsville is won by Confederacy; Stonewall Jackson is accidentally shot by his own troops.
May 22 – July 4
Union wins siege of Vicksburg in Mississippi.
June 3
Lee invades the North from Fredericksburg, Virginia.
July 3
Battle of Gettysburg is won in Pennsylvania by Union.
July 13 – 17
Riots occur in New York City over the draft.
November 19
Lincoln delivers the Gettysburg Address.

March 12
Grant becomes general-in-chief of Union army.
May 5 – 6
Lee and Lt. Gen. James Longstreet defeat Grant at the Wilderness Battle in Virginia.
May 6 – September 2
Atlanta Campaign ends in Union general William Tecumseh Sherman's occupation of Atlanta.
May 8 – 19
Lee and Grant maneuver for position in the Spotsylvania Campaign.
June 3
Grant is repelled at Cold Harbor, Virginia.
June 18, 1864 – April 2, 1865
Grant conducts the Siege of Petersburg, in Virginia, ending with evacuation of the city and Confederate withdrawal from Richmond.
August 5
Admiral Farragut wins Battle of Mobile Bay for Union.
October 6
Union general Philip Sheridan lays waste to Shenandoah Valley, Virginia, cutting off Confederacy's food supplies.
November 8
Lincoln is reelected president.
November 15 – December 13
Sherman's March to the Sea ends with Union occupation of Savannah, Georgia.

March 2
First Reconstruction Act is passed, reorganizing governments of Southern states.

| 1866 | 1867 | 1868 | 1869 |

April 9
Civil Rights Act of 1866 is passed. Among other things, it removes states' power to keep former slaves from testifying in court or owning property.

November 3
Ulysses S. Grant is elected president.

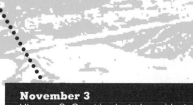

January 31
Thirteenth Amendment, freeing slaves, is passed by Congress and sent to states for ratification.
February 1 – April 26
Sherman invades the Carolinas.
February 6
Lee is appointed general-in-chief of Confederate armies.
March 3
Freedman's Bureau is established to assist former slaves.
April 9
Lee surrenders to Grant at Appomattox Courthouse, Virginia.
April 15
Lincoln dies from assassin's bullet; Andrew Johnson becomes president.
May 26
Remaining Confederate troops surrender.

A "Peculiarsome" Farmboy

"My best friend is the man who'll git me a book I
ain't read."

ABE LINCOLN, AGE ABOUT 12

On a cold day in the winter of 1816 a small wagon set off through the woods of Kentucky. It was pulled by two horses, and inside sat a husband and wife and their two young children. The father, a big, powerful man who looked like a wrestler, held the horses' reins. The little family traveled through wild lands, with bears roaming in the brush and cougars in the branches. The trees before them seemed to go on forever, an unending stretch of elm, beech, walnut, oak, and maple.

Eventually the family reached the wide Ohio River, where they boarded a ferry and crossed into the new state of Indiana. There they came upon a clearing near a babbling stream called Little Pigeon Creek. The trees around the clearing were marked white, and there were piles of brush in the corners. This was the place the father had marked before. Here they would make their home.

Abraham Lincoln, then seven years old, surveyed the landscape and found it to his liking. It was a good place for a cabin.

But for now there was no cabin, only trees and underbrush. Abe's father, Tom, and his mother, Nancy, both went to work. They cut sapling trunks into poles and lashed them together. Abe and his nine-year-old sister, Sarah, helped. Working quickly, the family soon built a "pole shed," a half-open shelter in which they would live until they could build a proper cabin.

Tom Lincoln had moved to Indiana in search of good land. He didn't have much money, so he became a "squatter." That meant that Tom would settle there and work the land. Eventually, after he paid two dollars an acre, the federal government would recognize him as the owner for the work he had put into the land. The United States of America was only 40 years old, and its citizens were not rich. They had a great deal of energy, however, and there were enormous tracts of land for them to explore and farm. Wagonloads of easterners were moving into the "wilderness" of the western frontier, which in those days meant the land that now includes the states of Illinois, Indiana, and Ohio. Indian tribes— from the Shawnee in the Ohio River Valley to the Creek and Cherokee farther south—were fighting losing struggles for their homelands. Many easterners wanted to settle on a piece of this good land. Tom Lincoln was one of them.

Tom had a good heart, but he was not a very successful man. He had worked several farms in Kentucky in the past, but he had never done a very good job of it. Now he had a fine piece of land and a chance to try again.

The cabin-building went slowly. When it was finally raised, the cabin was not a big one, or a particularly lovely one. In fact, it was rather crude, even by wilderness standards. It was only 18 by 18 feet. It had one room that served as living room, dining room, and kitchen. The floor was made of dirt, and a small platform overhead, reached by climbing pegs in the wall, served as the children's bedroom.

Still, the cabin seemed like a good, solid place to Abe, who had helped build it. He compared it favorably with his other home, the log cabin in Kentucky in which he was born.

Young Abraham Lincoln was tall for his age, with a long lanky frame and hands and feet that looked too big for him. Though he was still young, he was handy with all types of tools. But although the family depended on wild game for food in those early days, he had never learned to shoot a gun properly.

Then one day in February 1817, Abe was working alone on the cabin, which by then was nearly completed. All at once he spotted a flock of wild turkeys flying toward the cabin. He picked up his father's rifle, took aim, and fired. One of the birds sailed to earth, dead. But the boy took no pleasure in the kill. Later in life, looking back on the boy that he was, Abraham Lincoln said of himself, "He has never since pulled a trigger on any larger game." He would become many things, but a hunter was not one of them. He had no taste for killing.

After the Lincolns had lived nearly a year in their little cabin, friends arrived. Nancy's foster parents from Kentucky, Betsy and Tom Sparrow, had decided to make the trip to Indiana themselves. They brought with them Dennis Hanks, a boy whom they had adopted.

The new arrivals moved into the half-open pole shed the Lincolns had lived in while building the cabin. Abe and Dennis soon became great friends, though Dennis was 17 years old. He was an ungainly backwoods boy, and not known for cleverness, but he was also a colorful character. He did not like his temporary home very much. He called the pole shed a "darn little half-face camp."

Tom and Betsy Sparrow had come north hoping to find good land to farm and a better life for themselves. But they did not find it. Only a year after they had arrived, both of them fell ill. Abe's mother tended to them, wondering what could be wrong. Then she knew: their tongues were coated with a white, filmy substance. All pioneer families knew this as a sign of the dreaded milk sickness, a result of drinking milk from cows that had eaten the poisonous snakeroot plant. Within a month, they were both dead.

Another tragedy was soon to follow. To the horror of Abe and Sarah, their mother took to her bed with severe stomach pains. She, too, had the white film covering her tongue. In October 1818, Nancy Lincoln died.

It was a tremendous loss for the children. They had loved their mother dearly, and they were now alone in the wilderness with only their father and Dennis Hanks. Still, the death was a reality, and the children now had to perform tasks that adults usually did. Abe and Dennis helped Abe's father cut wood from a log into planks to build a coffin. Then the three of them dug a grave next to the graves of the Sparrows, and there they buried Nancy Lincoln.

It was the saddest period in young Abe Lincoln's life. He did not know what to expect next. What would happen to his family without a mother to cook, sew clothes, cure meats, churn butter, and do the hundred other things necessary in a pioneer farmhouse? Sarah was doing her best, but it was impossible for her to fill her mother's shoes. She was still a child and simply did not know how to do half the things she was supposed to do.

Less than a year later, Tom Lincoln made a decision. He packed up a horse and left the three children, telling them he would come back with a surprise. In December 1819 he returned, and with a very big surprise indeed. Abe and Sarah rushed out of the cabin just as a large wagon led by four horses rolled into the clearing. Inside was their father, with his new wife and her three children!

Tom Lincoln, realizing that his family needed a woman, had gone back to Kentucky and proposed marriage to Sarah Johnston, a widow whom he had known since they were children. "I have no wife and you no husband," he had said to her in his direct, gruff way. "I came a-purpose to marry you. I knowed you from a gal and you knowed me from a boy. I have no time to lose, and if you're willin' let it be done straight off."

Sarah Johnston agreed, and a short time later the one-room cabin in Indiana became home to eight people. Abe and Sarah quickly became fond of their new mother. They found her a sweet-tempered woman who, nevertheless, knew how to get things done—and there was plenty to be done around the cabin. There was almost no furniture, the roof had holes in it, and the children had only the poorest clothes. Years later Dennis Hanks said that in

the wintertime, instead of comfortable shoes, they wore "birch bark, with hickory bark soles, stropped on over yarn socks."

Within a short while, Sarah saw to repairs of the cabin. She set Tom and Dennis to work building proper chairs and a nice, solid table, while she and Abe's sister made good, sturdy clothing for the children to wear. Abe and his sister had been sleeping on a mat made of corn husks before their stepmother arrived. Now they had a nice feather bed, which she had brought with her.

The Lincoln children and the Johnston children got along well with each other. Abe and Dennis showed John Johnston around the "neighborhood," and the three boys worked side by side on the farm. Abe's sister Sarah became friends with John's two sisters, Matilda and Sarah Johnston. (There were now three Sarahs in the household. This was probably confusing at times. When Tom Lincoln called, "Sarah!" nobody would know whether he wanted his wife, his daughter, or his stepdaughter!)

The next task for the new Mrs. Lincoln was to see to the children's education. It was hard to find a teacher. Proper schools were rare in the territories and newly made states of the American West, and well-educated teachers were even rarer. Anyone who happened into the region and who could read and write was recruited to be teacher to all the children whose families wanted them to have schooling. (Many years later, Lincoln wrote, "If a straggler supposed to understand Latin happened to sojourn in [wander into] the neighborhood, he was looked upon as a wizard.") In payment, the families would send the new teacher bushels of corn and potatoes, hams, sides of venison, or whatever other food they had available. Trading food for work was common on the frontier, where money was often unavailable.

So the children had a variety of schoolteachers, each for only a short period. Therefore, they could have no fixed school year. They simply went to school whenever there was a teacher to teach them.

As far as Abraham was concerned, this was an easy chore. He enjoyed whatever schooling he could get, and he was happy to walk the four miles to the schoolhouse. Some of the schoolbooks he used were *Webster's Spelling Book*, *Murray's English Reader*, and *Pike's*

Arithmetic. Abe worked hard at arithmetic, scratching sums on rough sheets of paper. Occasionally he got bored, and instead of sums wrote rhymes:

> Abraham Lincoln is my name
> and with my pen I wrote the same.
> I wrote in both haste and speed
> and left it here for fools to read.

Still, the boy received most of his education from books he read at home. As he grew he developed a passion for reading. Before the fireplace in the cabin he once announced to his family, "My best friend is the man who'll git me a book I ain't read."

The books he was able to "git" included the Bible (which Abe liked very much, though he was never fond of the blustery country evangelists), *Robinson Crusoe,* and a book with the rather long title of *The Life of George Washington, with Curious Anecdotes, Equally Honorable to Himself and Exemplary to His Young Countrymen.* This

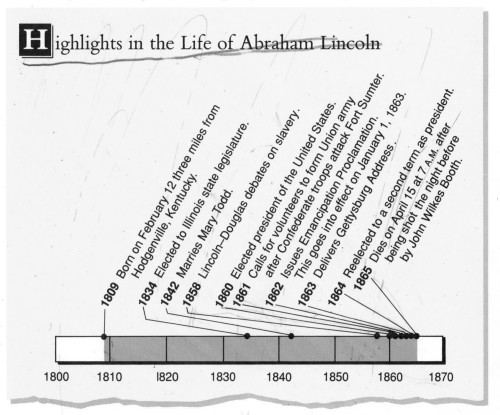

Highlights in the Life of Abraham Lincoln

- **1809** Born on February 12 three miles from Hodgenville, Kentucky.
- **1834** Elected to Illinois state legislature.
- **1842** Marries Mary Todd.
- **1858** Lincoln–Douglas debates on slavery.
- **1860** Elected president of the United States.
- **1861** Calls for volunteers to form Union army after Confederate troops attack Fort Sumter.
- **1862** Issues Emancipation Proclamation. This goes into effect on January 1, 1863.
- **1863** Delivers Gettysburg Address.
- **1864** Reelected to a second term as president.
- **1865** Dies on April 15 at 7 A.M. after being shot the night before by John Wilkes Booth.

1800   1810   1820   1830   1840   1850   1860   1870

last book was lent to him by a gruff old neighbor named Josiah Crawford. One night Abe left it on a table leaning against the log wall of the cabin. It rained all night, and in the morning the boy found the book soaking wet. Crawford demanded 75 cents in exchange. Abe did not have that kind of money, so instead he worked for three whole days picking fodder in Crawford's fields, at a rate of 25 cents a day.

Another book that Abe fell in love with was Aesop's *Fables*. In the evenings he would sit down before the fireplace with the other children and tell some of the stories to them, like the one about the wolf who put on a sheep's hide in order to trick a flock of sheep into letting him get near them. Some of the children liked hearing the stories, but Dennis Hanks burst out laughing once and said, "Abe, them yarns is all lies!" Abe Shrugged. "Might good lies, Denny," he said.

The boy seemed to care more about books than about the farm, which everyone thought most strange. But no one was more amazed at Abe's love of books than Dennis Hanks. The ungainly young man once said that people would sometimes come into the cabin while Abe was sitting against the chimney reading. A while later they would leave again, with Abe never knowing they were there, and say to themselves, "Well, I'll be darned." Dennis thought, "It didn't seem natural, nohow, to see a feller read like that." As Abe grew and his love of reading continued, Dennis remarked, "There's somethin' peculiarsome about Abe."

Young Abe had a good reason for wanting to read. It was not that he wanted to get out of doing work on the farm. He was strong and willing to do his share of chopping wood and plowing fields. But the young man knew that there was a whole world out there beyond the forests of Indiana, and he was on fire to find out about it. He gobbled up every fact he could about history, science, or literature.

Besides books there was another source of fascination for Abe when he was a teenager. The farm was close to the Ohio River, and he would often make his way down to the river to watch the goings-on. First there was the mighty river itself, so slow and stately and wide, moving along on its steady way. Then there were the people of the river. In those days the great rivers were like highways. Nearly all shipping of goods was by flatboat, and lots of passengers traveled the river in enormous steamboats. The towns along the banks were always bustling with activity as well. Abe took it all in.

In a way his two fascinations were the same. Books were one way for the young man to move beyond his small world to the infinitely greater one beyond. The river was another way. For a time Abe even made up his mind that he would become a steamboat man when he came of age.

At age 17 Abraham Lincoln was six feet two inches tall. He was lean, lanky, and strong—in fact, he was known far and wide as a wrestler. He had a firm face, but his skin, said one of the girls he went to school with, was "shriveled and yellow." She also said that he typically wore "buckskin breeches, a linsey-woolsey shirt, and a cap made of the skin of a squirrel or coon." So Abraham Lincoln was a backwoods boy indeed.

As he grew older, Abe became a great socializer. He loved to make his way down to the general store at the largest town in the region, Gentryville. There he would sit and listen to the old men tell stories, eventually chipping in his own contributions. When a traveling evangelist came to town, Abe watched him sway and swoon as he preached. The next day, Abe Lincoln was doing a hilarious imitation for the folks gathered at the store.

Abe now traveled far and wide in the area. He once walked 30 miles to the county courthouse. To him, lawyers and judges were the most educated of men, and he wanted to hear them in action. So he sat in the back of the courtroom for hours and watched the way the lawyers shook their fists as they argued their cases. He watched their faces go red as they got more and more excited. He listened to their carefully constructed arguments. When he got back home, he had a month of thinking to do about all he had heard. He had material for many sessions at the general store, where he would mimic the strutting and gesturing of the lawyers to the amusement of the local farmers.

But life was not all fun and games. There were sad times, too. Abe's sister, Sarah, had married, and in 1828 she died giving birth

to her first child. Abe was stung by the loss of his sister, with whom he had grown up. After he got over the shock, he noticed that he felt different. He was a man now. His childhood was behind him.

By the time he had reached his twentieth birthday, Abe was longing to get on with his life. Though he was not sure what sort of career he would seek, he was ready to strike out on his own. However, he could not simply abandon his family. His father had come to depend on him at the farm, and Abe felt his duty was to his family.

Then, in 1830, change came. Tom Lincoln had not been doing well with the farm. He had heard about richer lands to be had farther west, and he came home one day to announce that he had sold the cabin and the land. The family was picking up stakes and going to Illinois. It meant a new land for Abe to explore and new people for him to meet.

THE ODD-JOB MAN

"Fellow citizens, I presume you all know who I
am. I am humble Abraham Lincoln."

EARLY CAMPAIGN SPEECH

braham Lincoln had not been long in his new home before
he got a taste of a profession that was to his liking. The
family now lived on a farm on the edge of the prairie about
10 miles from the town of Decatur, Illinois. The farm was on the
banks of the Sangamon River, and here again Abe fell in love with
river life. He saw the river not only as a way to escape from the
drudgery of farm life, but as an important means of communication for the settlers.

One day, not long after the Lincoln family had settled into their
new home, Abe happened to be in Decatur to get supplies. With
him was his second cousin, John Hanks, Dennis Hanks's stepbrother. John had also moved to Illinois. They came upon a scene
that was entirely new to Abe. A man stood on a wooden crate next
to the general store lecturing a crowd.

The man, Abe learned, was a candidate for the Illinois legislature. Ever since he was a boy, Abe had been fascinated by public
speakers, whether they were lawyers, preachers, or just old men
holding forth at the general store. Also, being a bright young man,
Abe was immediately interested in the argument the candidate was
giving about why voters should choose him.

John Hanks whispered to Abe that this was the worst speech
he'd ever heard, and he said he was sure Abe could do better. The

candidate was talking about navigation on the Sangamon River. This was a subject about which Abe felt strongly.

Suddenly John turned over a crate and looked at Abe. Before he knew what he was doing, Abe Lincoln found himself standing on the crate next to the candidate. He began talking about the river. If canals were dug near the mouth of the river, Abe said, the water would not back up into farmers' fields anymore. Crops would no longer be endangered. Also, navigation on the river would improve.

People in the crowd nodded their heads. They eyed the young newcomer carefully. Abe jumped down off the crate. The candidate approached him. As John Hanks said later, "The man, after Abe's speech was through, took him aside and asked him where he had learned so much and how he could do so well. Abe replied, stating his manner and method of reading, and what he had read. The man encouraged him to persevere."

Abe determined that he would persevere, for he felt a pleasant jitteriness inside after his first public speech, a warm and exciting feeling. He liked it very much.

Abe helped his family to settle into its new farm. He split logs, tilled the hard midwestern soil, fenced the fields, helped build a barn and a smokehouse, where meat was cured, and did many other things. He helped to see the family through their first hard winter.

When spring came, though, he announced that it was time for him to strike out on his own. Abe was 22 years old. It was a wide world, and he wanted to see some of it.

John Hanks knew a man named Denton Offutt, who owned and operated riverboats. John came to Abe one day with a proposition: the two of them, along with Abe's stepbrother John Johnston, would be paid to build a flatboat for Offutt. They would load it with cargo and sail it down the Sangamon and Illinois rivers to the Mississippi. Then they would take that mighty river all the way to New Orleans—700 miles to the south.

Abe jumped at the chance. He had been to New Orleans a few years before, but only for a short time. This would be his chance to really see the big city. In late April of 1831, with the sweet smells of springtime in the air and newly budding leaves and flowers dotting the banks, the three young men set off down the river. Barrels of corn and salted pork were their cargo.

The eager crew passed St. Louis, Missouri, and made brief stops in Memphis, Tennessee, and Vicksburg, Mississippi. Coming into New Orleans at last, the young men were amazed by all they saw. To begin with, New Orleans was a big port town in those days. There was so much river traffic that they had to walk nearly a mile from one flatboat to the next before they reached land.

The city itself was also strange to the country boys. It contained 15,000 people, more than Abe Lincoln could ever have hoped to see in one place. All manner of houses, from tumbledown shacks to fine mansions, gleamed in the sun. There were so many streets that Abe could not figure out how a person got around the city without becoming hopelessly lost.

In the market streets, Abe was struck by the great variety of items for sale. There were pots and pans, fancy china, Asian silk, guns, toys, perfumes, and special lotions and potions that claimed to cure anything that might ail a person.

There was also one other "item" for sale in New Orleans. Abe and John Johnston came upon an auction block where a fat man stood in front of a black woman. He made her turn around so that the crowd gathered could see the muscles on her back. She would be a fine worker, he said. He opened her mouth to show a set of strong white teeth. She's in perfect health, he said. She will make an excellent worker, he said, and will have many babies who will grow into strong workers themselves. Then he opened the bidding.

Abe and John left the slave auction without speaking a word to one another. They walked through narrow streets filled with beggars, filthy children, drunken sailors, and ailing old people. They went back to their boarding room and decided it was time to leave New Orleans. All in all, they did not much like what they had seen.

For the next six years Abe Lincoln worked at a variety of jobs in and around his new hometown of New Salem, just north of

Springfield, Illinois. For a while he was the town postmaster, which helped him get to know many of the residents. Another advantage of this job was that he got to read all the newspapers that came into the office before they were delivered. In this way he began to learn about events in the state capital at Vandalia and in Washington, D.C.

He also worked in a store in town. Here he developed a reputation for honesty that would stay with him the rest of his life. Once, a woman paid too much for her order. Abe locked up the store and walked six miles after her to give her her change. Another time he accidentally used a lighter weight to measure some grain that a woman was buying. Again he closed the shop, sought out the woman, and made amends.

Eventually that store closed down, and Abe became part owner of another one across town. Not long afterward the owner died, leaving $1,100 in debts. Abe Lincoln lay awake at night thinking of all the money he owed. He arranged a payment plan and paid the money off a little at a time. It took him several years, but he finally erased all the debts.

Being an odd-job man was not all that Abe was doing in those years. He spent a great part of his waking hours studying. One day, Mentor Graham, the local schoolteacher, told him that a man who lived several miles down the road had a copy of an English grammar book. Abe had always felt insecure about his English, believing that he spoke like a backwoodsman (which he did). Now was his chance to learn some proper speech. He walked the whole way to the man's house, borrowed the book, and studied it every night to improve himself.

He also studied law at this time, and he read many great books of politics and history, such as *The History of the Decline and Fall of the Roman Empire*. As he read, he applied the principles he learned to the people of New Salem. What was right for large nations and empires, he figured, ought to be just as right for a small town. He often met with the local justice of the peace, or judge, whose name was Bowling Green, to discuss points of law. Green helped him to apply his knowledge by allowing Lincoln to write out arguments and decisions for some of his cases. Abe Lincoln, without any formal training, was becoming a lawyer simply by reading and "practicing."

It was not all work for Abe in New Salem. Not long after his arrival he met a gentle, fair-skinned girl with long, reddish-brown hair. She was one of the most popular girls in the town, full of fun and interested in everything. Her name was Ann Rutledge. Ann was well-known for her expert needlework, and Abe often walked her to "quilting bees," where women would meet and sew quilts. The two saw more and more of each other as time passed.

Years later, some of Abe's friends insisted that he and Ann Rutledge had become engaged at this time. His future law partner, William Herndon, claimed that Ann Rutledge had written to her brother, "As soon as his studies are completed we are to be married."

Meanwhile, Abe was to make a different kind of decision. He had long since recognized that he had a talent for public speaking. This, combined with his study of the law and his passion for honesty, brought him to the conclusion that politics would be a good career for him.

For some time now he had been attending town meetings and had kept up with state politics through the newspapers. He knew that he was well-known and well-liked in the area. His tall, gangly form loping through the streets was a common sight. He was respected for his honesty and liked for his storytelling ability. For all of these reasons, politics seemed a natural choice.

So, on a spring day in 1832, Abe Lincoln stood on a wooden platform before a group of local citizens and gave a short, simple speech:

"Fellow citizens, I presume you all know who I am. I am humble Abraham Lincoln. I have been solicited by many friends to become a candidate for the [Illinois state] legislature. My politics are short and sweet, like the old woman's dance. I am in favor of a national bank. I am in favor of the internal improvement system [projects such as roads and canals to improve transportation within the nation], and a high protective tariff. These are my sentiments and political principles. If elected I shall be thankful; if not it will be all the same."

A man who heard one of Lincoln's first political speeches said, "He was a very tall and gawky and rough looking fellow then. His pantaloons didn't meet his shoes by six inches. But after he began speaking, I became very much interested in him. He made a very sensible speech."

Of course, not everyone in the district knew who Abe Lincoln was. He would have to campaign hard to get elected. But, as things turned out, he would not be able to campaign much at all.

At this time, the government decided to do something once and for all about the tribes of Native Americans who were living in the area. These tribes were the Sac and the Fox. Years before, General William Henry Harrison had tricked them into selling their lands to the United States government. Federal troops drove them farther west, across the Mississippi River.

But these American Indians did not wish to give up the land on which their ancestors had lived and died. Their chief, Black Hawk, led his people eastward back across the river, where they began planting corn. "Land cannot be sold," Black Hawk declared angrily. "Nothing can be sold but such things as can be carried away."

The leaders of the state of Illinois did not take kindly to this behavior. The government ordered all able-bodied men to enlist in order to fight what came to be known as Black Hawk's War. Abraham Lincoln enlisted. He was given the title of captain and he commanded a small company of Illinois volunteers.

However, the "war" was soon over, for the scattered Native Americans were no match for the settlers. The wide homelands of the Sac and the Fox were now United States territory for good. In fact, the fighting was over before Captain Lincoln's company fought a single battle.

Still, by the time Lincoln left the army, it was too late for him to do much campaigning. When election day rolled around, he had spent very few days making himself known to the voters in his district. He lost the election.

He was not especially hurt by his loss, for he felt that he had not given it his full effort. He knew he would try again in two years. In the meantime, Lincoln worked at several more jobs. Most notably, he worked for a time as a land surveyor. The area was expanding rapidly. There was lots of work to support an intelligent young man who could help to mark out the boundaries of the new communities that were springing up. So Abe studied technical books until he was expert at the job.

Lincoln soon developed a reputation for being an excellent land surveyor who always measured boundaries accurately. But this was not entirely true. Many years later, the citizens of a town near New Salem were having a fight over properly lines. It seemed that there was a mistake, but nobody could figure out quite what the problem was.

Then an old man who lived nearby straightened things out. It seemed that years earlier he was working as an assistant to the surveyor who laid out the town. This surveyor was troubled when he found that if he drew this boundary line properly it would cut right into a poor man's house. "It's all he's got in the world, and he could never get another," the man remembered the surveyor saying. "I reckon it won't hurt anything out here if I skew the line a little and miss him."

Of course, the surveyor was Abraham Lincoln.

Lincoln worked as a surveyor, he later wrote, only "to keep body and soul together." He was biding his time until the next election. Then, in the spring of 1834, he announced that he would once again become a candidate for the Illinois state legislature.

This time he campaigned hard. In those days, rival candidates often went on a tour of the district, debating one another in town after town. Abe Lincoln had a problem, however. He had almost no money and could not possibly afford a horse and carriage. At the last moment, his opponent, Robert Wilson, saved the day by offering to allow Lincoln to ride with him.

Lincoln deeply appreciated Wilson's generosity, and he let others know about it. At the end of his speech, he told the audience:

"I am too poor to own a carriage, but my friend has generously invited me to ride with him. I want you to vote for me if you will. But if not then vote for my opponent, for he is a fine man."

The people of New Salem voted for Lincoln on election day. So did others around the district. When the votes were tallied, Abraham Lincoln had won a seat in the Illinois General Assembly. A new career had begun.

GROWING PAINS

"Emancipate the slave, and what then! He would
fiddle, steal, and then starve."

THEOPHILUS FISK, RADICAL LEADER

"We are the nation of human progress...."

JOHN L. SULLIVAN, NEWSPAPER EDITOR

Lincoln entered politics at a tense time. The United States was still a young country, and it was having growing pains that threatened to tear it apart. New political parties had formed to debate the issues of the day. But one issue was so explosive that no party knew how to deal with it. Slavery was the most talked-about, hotly argued problem of the age.

Lincoln began his political career as a member of the Whig party. This was a new party that rose to challenge the stronger Democratic-Republican party, which later became known as simply the Democratic party. Almost since the founding of the nation, there had been two major political parties. In the early days they were the Federalists, led by Alexander Hamilton, and the Anti-Federalists, led by Thomas Jefferson. The Federalists believed that the national government should be strong and that it should have power over the states, such as the power to create a national bank or the power to levy a tax on whiskey. The Anti-Federalists were worried that if the federal government got too much power it would be as dangerous as the English monarchy, which they had all fought so hard to overthrow. They emphasized individual and state rights over federal power.

31

Over the next few decades, the two parties moved closer together. By 1828 there almost was no two-party system. The members of Congress formed themselves into different groups who allied with one another to pass legislation. The presidents of this time—James Madison, James Monroe, and John Quincy Adams—were all wealthy, aristocratic men who had little in common with ordinary Americans. They and the leaders in Congress formed a government that was like a club: its members sometimes fought with one another but eventually decided things for themselves. This did not leave much room for the American people to have a say in their government.

Then, in 1828, a Tennessee frontiersman and former war hero, Andrew Jackson, was elected president. Powerful men in Washington were stunned. Presidents had always come from their ranks. Many thought that Jackson, the outsider, was the first president ever elected who would act to solve problems facing the ordinary people. To many Americans he seemed more honest and tough-minded than the Washington leaders. They liked his rough-and-ready style, his military background, and his frontier origins. Jackson was also the first president from the western states. This was an indication that the West was now a powerful force in national politics, perhaps as powerful as the South and the North.

Jackson was part of a new political party, called the Democratic party. The Democrats, who grew out of Jefferson's Anti-Federalists, believed in "government by the people." They did not agree with the old Federalists like Noah Webster, who said that "the man who has half a million dollars in property...has a much higher interest in government than the man who has little or no property." Many Federalists believed only the few wealthy property owners in the nation should be allowed to vote.

The Federalist party had died out by the time Jackson's Democrats came into being. In time, however, President Jackson's power grew so great that many leaders feared him. They called him "King Andrew," and they decided to oppose him. They formed the Whig party in 1834. The party's leaders were Henry Clay and Daniel Webster. In its early days, the party worked mostly to try to limit the president's power. Later they developed a program favoring a strong national government and supporting such "internal improvements" as building railroads.

When Abraham Lincoln entered his first political office as a Whig, his heroes were Clay and Webster. He liked President Jackson's fondness for the "common man," but he did not care for many of the president's policies.

Henry Clay, founder of the Whig party, strongly supported federal aid for public works projects.

Jackson did not support the idea of a national bank, which would help to finance businesses in the West. Lincoln believed a national bank was necessary if his own state of Illinois was to grow and prosper. He was determined that the government would help the citizens of the newly settled lands build factories, roads, and bridges. The nation would continue to expand, and this was the only way it could stay together.

One of the greatest issues that the new parties, and individual citizens, had to face was slavery. Decades before, many citizens of the United States believed that slavery was an evil that would eventually die out. It was the growth of industry in the nation that would cause opinions to change.

Thanks to the cotton gin, a machine that could remove seeds from cotton, vast new areas of the South and Southwest opened up to cotton farming. Factories in European nations and in New England eagerly bought up as much cotton as the South could produce. The cotton plantations got bigger and bigger to meet the demand. As they did, they needed more and more slaves. By 1820 there were 1,500,000 slaves in the Southern states, most working on huge plantations.

Now, in the 1830s, although few Southern whites actually owned slaves, many Southerners could not see how they could ever do without slavery. They believed slaves were necessary to their economic survival. They did not think it was possible for the plantations to prosper with paid laborers.

In 1820 the Congress discussed admitting Missouri to the Union. Some members wanted it to be admitted as a "free state," one in which slavery would not be legal. This was not because Northerners were better people. The climate was different in the North, and it was more profitable to hire laborers during the short growing season than to keep slaves. So, in a way, it was easier for Northerners to be "moral" about slavery, since most of them did not benefit by it.

Southerners insisted that Missouri be a "slave state" instead. Tempers flared, newspapers hurled accusations, and streetcorner fights broke out over the slavery question. Finally, a compromise was worked out. Missouri would become a slave state, but a line was drawn at its southern border. All lands south of this line could be admitted as slave states when their turn came, while all lands to the north—except Missouri itself—would become free states. Maine became the next free state, keeping the number of free states and slave states equal.

Many people thought the Missouri Compromise, as it came to be known, finally solved the problem of slavery, at least in the Louisiana Territory. But in fact the members of the government hadn't solved anything. They had merely found a way to delay coming to terms with the issue. Many thinkers realized the slavery issue was so powerful that it could split the country in two.

By the 1830s, when Abe Lincoln was still a member of the Illinois state legislature, slavery affected state, as well as national, politics. In 1837, Elijah Lovejoy, a newspaper man in Illinois, was murdered by an angry mob. Lovejoy had been an abolitionist, someone who argued that the nation had a moral duty to free all slaves immediately and to abolish slavery. The mob destroyed his printing press, then killed him. The legislature proposed resolutions to deal with the situation. However, instead of punishing the mob, the resolutions stated that abolitionist groups should be outlawed because they incited the public to riot. The idea of free speech was now under attack.

Abraham Lincoln voted against the resolutions. He gave an angry speech to a citizens' group. He said that the United States had been formed so that people could express their opinions freely, without fear of harm. The country would not last, he said, if angry mobs were allowed to "burn churches, ravage and rob provision stores, throw printing presses into rivers, shoot editors, and hang and burn obnoxious [offensive] persons at pleasure, and with impunity [without fear of punishment]; depend on it, this Government cannot last."

Lincoln was not an abolitionist himself. He often said he believed slavery was an evil institution that must eventually end if the country was to survive. But he did not openly call for the government to abolish it. Instead, he argued for slavery to be limited to the Southern states and gradually eliminated.

YOUNG MAN ON THE RISE

"A girl might be born and become a mother before the Van Buren men will forget Mr. Lincoln."

AN ILLINOIS NEWSPAPER, ON
THE ELECTION OF 1836

The town of Vandalia, Illinois, was a primitive place for a state capital. Its main street was a dirt road lined with log cabins and a few larger frame houses. It sat on the banks of the Kaskaskia River surrounded by forest. Vandalia had saloons that filled with rowdies in the evening, and one big jailhouse for troublemakers.

Stagecoaches rumbled into town regularly on their way farther west or to the big cities of the East. One day late in November 1834, the stagecoach carrying several newly elected members of the state legislature pulled into town. One of them was a tall, gaunt young man wearing a new $60 suit. The pants did not quite reach his shoes. The young legislator did not have money to spend on a suit, but a friend in New Salem, Coleman Smoot, had loaned him $200 so that he could begin his career in proper style.

Later a story would go around that Abe Lincoln was so poor at the time that he walked the 75 miles from New Salem to Vandalia. When he heard it, Abe smiled and said, "No harm, if true; but, in fact, not true."

Although Vandalia was a simple town, it seemed a high-class place to Abe. Here were lawyers and politicians from all over the state. The drawing rooms of the boarding houses where they lived had fine furnishings. Many members of the state legislature brought their wives and daughters. The men thought the women enlivened the society with their sparkling talk and frilly finery. Elaborate parties were given where members mingled, toasted one another, and discussed the important issues of the day.

The Illinois legislature got down to business on December 1. Abraham Lincoln had a seat at a small table near the back of the room. It was a large, drafty place, as crude as the town. In the center of the floor was a sandpit to be used by members as a spittoon (for spitting tobacco).

The issues the legislature faced were those of a young and fast-growing state. The Industrial Revolution and the expansion of the United States were bringing rapid changes to the former wilderness. Members introduced bills to incorporate a state bank, to build state roads, to fund the railroad, and to recognize new towns.

Abe Lincoln did little talking during his first session in the legislature. He listened a great deal and cast his votes with care. Early in his term (the two years for which he was elected), he introduced a bill granting a friend in New Salem the right to construct a bridge over Salt Creek. He was pleased when the Illinois House of Representatives passed it.

Late in the session, Lincoln relaxed and showed his fellow legislators a bit of his humor. The House had selected a man named Samuel McHatton to replace the land surveyor of Schuyler County, who had died. Then came news that the old surveyor had not died after all. The members of the House were trying to decide what to do when Abe Lincoln rose and suggested they keep Mr. McHatton as their choice. That way, he said, gently mocking the formal speech used in the legislature, "if the old surveyor should hereafter conclude to die, there would be a new one ready without troubling the legislature." The members chuckled and agreed to his plan.

When the legislative session ended in February, Lincoln returned to New Salem. He picked up his surveying tools and went to work again, for the pay of a legislator was not enough to cover expenses. Lincoln still needed the money that surveying brought.

He also returned to his study of the law. He was determined to pass the state bar examination the following year, which would make him eligible to practice law in Illinois.

Later that summer Lincoln got bad news. On August 25, 1835, Ann Rutledge died of a fever that doctors of the time called "brain fever." Abe Lincoln went into shock. No one today knows how close he and Ann Rutledge were, but Ann's cousin later wrote that Abe "took her death [very] hard."

For a long time afterward, Abe expressed little interest in women. In 1836 he proposed marriage to Mary Owens, the sister-in-law of one of his New Salem friends. But he seemed to do it because he felt it was time to marry, not because he loved her. Mary Owens turned him down, and Abe appeared to give up on the idea of marriage.

At about this time, Lincoln's term as legislator was finished. He ran for reelection with a passion his friends had never yet seen in him. Being a Whig, Lincoln was still opposed to the policies of President Andrew Jackson. The year was 1836, which was also a presidential election year, and Jackson's successor in the Democratic party was Martin Van Buren, whom the Whigs disliked. One day, before a large crowd in Springfield, Lincoln gave a stirring speech about what members of the Whig party believed.

One person in the audience was a lawyer named George Forquer, a Whig who had switched to the Democratic party in exchange for being named registrar of the Land Office. Besides being known for this sudden switch, Forquer was also known as the first man in the area to erect a lightning rod on his house. Forquer stood up following Lincoln's speech and gave one of his own. He said that young Abe Lincoln would have to be "taken down." He argued against every point Lincoln had made.

When Forquer finished, Lincoln again took the stage. A friend of his later said, "I have heard him often since, in the courts and before the people, but never saw him appear and acquit himself so well as upon that occasion." Lincoln responded powerfully, and finished: "I desire to live, and I desire place and distinction; but I would rather die now than, like the gentleman, live to see the day that I would change my politics for an office worth three thousand dollars a year, and then feel compelled to erect a lightning rod to protect a guilty conscience from an offended God."

The crowd hooted and cheered. Lincoln left that day a more famous man than before. One of the local papers said, "A girl might be born and become a mother before the Van Buren men will forget Mr. Lincoln." Forquer was much talked about, too, though not in a way that pleased him.

On election day, Abraham Lincoln was reelected by an overwhelming margin. Nationally, however, the Democrats were the winners, and Martin Van Buren became the country's eighth president. Still, this was an important day for the Whig party in Sangamon County. The county had always been controlled by Democrats in the state government, but after the 1836 election all seven of the county's representatives to the House and both its representatives in the Senate would be Whigs. It happened that all nine of these newly elected men were rather tall. When the new legislature met in Vandalia, they were called the "Long Nine."

The Long Nine tended to vote together and became very influential. One of them later joked, "All the bad or [unpleasant] laws passed at that session of the Legislature and for many years afterwards were chargeable to the management and influence of the 'Long Nine.'"

On September 9, 1836, Abraham Lincoln passed the bar examination and was finally admitted to practice law in the state of Illinois. He joined the law firm headed by John T. Stuart. He also put aside his surveying tools. He would never need to use them again.

Soon afterward, the legislature voted to move the state capital from Vandalia to the larger town of Springfield. Springfield was a bustling market town that supplied goods to people from all over the county. It was also where John Stuart's law firm was located. So, in the springtime of 1837, Abraham Lincoln arrived, carrying all his belongings in his saddlebags.

His first business was to find a place to stay. He told the owner of the general store, Joshua Speed, that he needed a room but that he had hardly any money. Speed later said, "The tone of his voice was so melancholy that I felt for him." Speed invited the lanky traveler to stay with him until he found a better place.

A big smile spread across Abe Lincoln's weary face. He dashed upstairs, flung his saddlebags down, and returned saying, "Well, Speed, I'm moved."

Lincoln had known his law partner, John Stuart, since the days of Black Hawk's War. Stuart had helped Lincoln make it through his studies and now welcomed the young lawyer to his office, which was located in the same building as the new legislature. The office was not much: a small room with a wood-burning stove, a table, and some bookshelves. But Lincoln was as eager as could be.

Stuart was at this time running for Congress, which meant that the young lawyer got to handle most of the legal cases that came in. Lincoln gained a great deal of experience in a short time. Not only did he handle the cases, but he also managed the office. The account books still exist, written in Lincoln's careful hand. He also traveled "the circuit." Along with other lawyers and judges, Abe rode from town to town throughout the county. In each town a stack of cases would be waiting for trial.

There was a great variety of these cases. Some involved complex complaints against the government. Some were simple domestic matters. One of Lincoln's first cases was the defense of a young man who had killed a man in a drunken fight. Lincoln lost the case, and the man was hanged.

Another murder case became much more famous. Lincoln and Stuart together defended Henry Truett, a politician who had shot and killed his opponent, Jacob Early, in an argument. Lincoln pointed out to the jury that Early had picked up a chair and was about to attack Truett with it. So, Lincoln argued, Truett acted out of self-defense. The jury agreed.

Not all of Lincoln's cases were so violent. Most involved drawing up a last will and testament or having legal documents signed. Once a man named Ross came to Lincoln with a paper that needed a judge's signature. It was Saturday, and Lincoln knew that the judge would be in his farm fields. Lincoln and Ross found the judge busily building a hog pen. They got him to sign the papers. Lincoln said they were holding a "shirt-sleeve court," since they were all dressed in working clothes. The judge laughed. Lincoln then offered to help build the pen. He and Ross worked alongside the judge, and the judge decided that in exchange for their help he would not charge a fee. Springfield may have been an uppity state capital to some, but to others it was a down-home country town where folks helped each other. Lincoln seemed to be right at home.

One of the Long Nine was Ninian Edwards, a refined man who lived with his wife, Elizabeth, in a large and impressive house on the outskirts of Springfield. Both of them came from upper-class families and were used to the finer things in life.

In 1839, Elizabeth's sister, Mary Todd, moved from her home in Kentucky to stay with them. Mary was an even more refined society woman than her sister. She held herself erect, wore fancy gowns, danced beautifully, spoke French, and considered Europe to be the home of all things civilized. She was a cultured 21-year-old, with flashing eyes and a strong personality. In no time she had caught the eye of several of the young lawyers and politicians in the state capital. She held her own at parties, discussing the issues of the day and showing everyone that she could read the characters of all the important leaders.

Many young men fell in love with her. One man, William Herndon, whose father was one of the Long Nine, met her at a ball. "I engaged her for a waltz," he later said, "and as we glided through it I fancied I never before had danced with a young lady who moved with such grace and ease."

Mary Todd was also an ambitious woman. Her sister once said, "She loved show and power, and was the most ambitious woman I ever knew. She used to contend when a girl, to her friends in Kentucky, that she was destined to marry a president."

One of the many young men who met her was Abraham Lincoln. His friend Joshua Speed, who knew Ninian Edwards well, brought Lincoln to the Edwards house. Lincoln had long ago given up on the idea of marriage, but he was fascinated by this young woman. He had never met a woman before who could handle herself so well in company with men. She was more like the high society women of the big East Coast cities, such as New York or Washington, D.C. A backwoods lawyer like Lincoln did not know what to make of her. But he was interested.

Lincoln came to the Edwards house many times to be with Mary. Mary's sister later said, "I have often happened in the room where they were sitting, and Mary invariably led the conversation. Mr. Lincoln would sit at her side and listen. He scarcely said a word, but gazed on her as if irresistibly drawn towards her by some superior and unseen power."

Within a short time Abe Lincoln and Mary Todd were planning to marry. Then, suddenly, a problem arose. A young dandy named Stephen Douglas, whom Lincoln knew well from political circles, suddenly began attracting Mary. Douglas was a short man with a very dignified manner. Where Lincoln was rough and homespun and humorous, Douglas had a smooth, noble bearing. Lincoln would see him walking down the street with Mary, the two of them arm in arm. Abe Lincoln was more bewildered than ever.

At last Mary Todd broke off her relationship with Douglas. She was now free to marry Abe. But Lincoln had decided it would be better for him to avoid her. She had a strange power over him. He liked being with her, but then again he did not.

However, when he went to break off his engagement, things did not work as he had planned. He told Speed later that when he told Mary he did not love her, she burst into tears and began wringing her hands.

"What else did you say?" asked Speed.

"To tell you the truth, Speed," Lincoln replied, "it was too much for me. I found the tears trickling down my own cheeks. I caught her in my arms and kissed her."

Speed could not believe it. "And that's how you broke the engagement?" he cried.

Lincoln shrugged. Things remained confused for the next year. Finally, late in 1842, the two decided once again to marry—and quickly.

On the morning of November 4, 1842, the tall form of Abe Lincoln appeared at the foot of James Matheny's bed. Matheny was a close friend of Abe's. "I'm going to be married today," Abe said. He asked Matheny to be his best man. He and Mary were to be married that evening.

Next Abe met Ninian Edwards and told him. Edwards insisted that the wedding must take place at his house. Quickly guests were informed, and the minister was found. That evening, at long last, Abraham Lincoln married Mary Todd.

No one knows for certain why there was so much trouble surrounding the marriage. Many people think Lincoln was half in love with Mary Todd and half afraid of her. Others say he finally married her only to keep his honor, for he had offered to marry her the year before. Whatever the case, Lincoln himself was as confused as anyone. Shortly after the wedding he wrote to a fellow lawyer, "Nothing new here, except my marrying, which to me, is a matter of profound wonder."

5

ON TO WASHINGTON

"I never saw so many words compressed into so small an idea."

CONGRESSMAN LINCOLN, ON AN EMPTY
SPEECH IN THE HOUSE OF REPRESENTATIVES

By 1844 Lincoln had established his own law practice. He had left John Stuart's firm and opened his own office. His partner was William Herndon, the enthusiastic young lawyer who had once danced with Mary Todd at the Edwards house, and whose father was one of the Long Nine.

William Herndon had only recently passed his bar examination and was nervous about becoming Lincoln's partner. "I was young in the practice and was painfully aware of my want of ability and experience," he later wrote, "but when he remarked in his earnest, honest way, 'Billy, I can trust you, if you can trust me,' I felt relieved, and accepted the generous proposal."

Herndon remained Lincoln's law partner for the rest of his life, even after Lincoln entered the White House. Herndon said, "It has always been a matter of pride with me that during our long partnership...we never had any personal controversy or disagreement."

The law practice of Lincoln and Herndon grew. Abe and Mary Lincoln moved from a boardinghouse to a home of their own. In

August 1843 their first child was born, a son whom they named Robert Todd Lincoln.

But Abe Lincoln was not completely content. He had served three terms in the Illinois legislature and now was after a bigger prize. He wanted to run for Congress of the United States.

This would not be easy. That year, 1844, the Whig party had nominated Edward Baker to run for representative of Lincoln's district. Baker was well-known and well-liked. He was also a friend of Lincoln's. In fact, he was such a good friend that when Abe and Mary's second son was born in August of 1846 they named the boy Edward Baker Lincoln.

So, rather than battle a good friend and probably lose, Lincoln decided not to run. Instead, he became a presidential elector—one of the men who are chosen by the people in a presidential election year to vote on their behalf for a certain candidate.

Lincoln was an elector for Henry Clay, the great Whig leader, who was running against James Polk in the election of 1844. He felt strongly that Clay must win the presidency. If elected, Polk promised to bring Texas into the Union and to take Oregon from Great Britain. Clay and the Whigs opposed this muscle-bound kind of policy. So did Lincoln.

Lincoln crisscrossed the state of Illinois on behalf of Clay. But he was also campaigning for himself. He was meeting important citizens who could help him later. For Abraham Lincoln had already decided that in the next election, in 1846, he would run for Congress.

The 1844 election was a disaster for the Whigs. James Polk defeated Henry Clay. Some Whigs were so upset that they declared they would not cut their hair or shave again until Henry Clay was made president. William Herndon later wrote that, 36 years after the election, he saw one ornery old man with long hair and beard who was still living up to his promise!

By the time the 1846 election race rolled around, Lincoln was ready to run for office. He received the Whig nomination for a seat in the U.S. House of Representatives, the lower house of Congress. Now he faced the Democratic candidate, a blustery, old-fashioned

This photo was taken in 1846, the year Lincoln was elected to the House of Representatives.

country evangelist named Peter Cartwright. Cartwright was popular with the backwoods people of Lincoln's district. He would be hard to beat.

The tough, bull-necked Cartwright came out swinging. His first shot was the fact that Lincoln was not a member of a church congregation. He spread rumors: Lincoln was unfaithful to his wife; Lincoln did not believe in Jesus Christ.

Lincoln was furious at these low campaign tactics. He finally published a statement of his religious views to put the matter to rest. "That I am not a member of any Christian church is true," he wrote, "but I have never denied the truth of the Scriptures."

Later, Lincoln attended one of Cartwright's prayer meetings. "Brother" Cartwright waved his arms, thundered warnings, and rolled his eyes. Finally he asked that all who wished to be saved should stand up. Many people did. Next he asked that everyone who did not wish to go to hell stand up. Everyone in the hall stood except one man. Abraham Lincoln sat grimly in his seat, his eyes fixed on the preacher. Cartwright's eyes lit up. He pointed an accusing finger and said, "May I inquire of you, Mr. Lincoln, where you are going?"

Lincoln scanned the crowd. "I came here as a respectful listener," he said. "I did not know that I was to be singled out by Brother Cartwright. I believe in treating religious matters with due solemnity... Brother Cartwright asks me directly where I am going. I desire to reply with equal directness: I am going to Congress."

The citizens liked Abe Lincoln's direct manner, his experience, and his gentle humor. They elected him their representative by a wide margin. When the election was over, Lincoln made public his campaign expenses. Friends had lent him $200. He returned $199.25. He said, "I did not need the money. I made the canvass [visits to towns to ask for votes] on my own horse; my entertainment, being at the houses of my friends, cost me nothing. My only outlay was 75 cents for a barrel of cider which some farmhands insisted I should treat [them] to."

At last, in December 1847, Abraham Lincoln arrived in Washington, D.C. The members of Congress welcomed the tall, awkward-looking man with the stovepipe hat stuffed with papers, the wrinkled clothes, and the sad smile. He immediately entered the debate on the hottest question of the day: war.

Following James Polk's election promise, the United States had declared war on Mexico the year before. The country's quest for land was unstoppable, even though it had grown enormously. When Lincoln was born, the United States had 5 million citizens living in 16 states. By 1846 it had 20 million people and 26 states.

But it was not enough. Some people came to believe that the United States had a divine right to conquer the whole continent, from sea to sea. A newspaper editor called it "manifest destiny," and the phrase caught on. Texas, which had been part of Mexico until 1836, was admitted to the Union in 1845. Now, one year later, President Polk decided he wanted the territory that comprised what are today the states of Utah, Nevada, and California, and parts of Arizona, New Mexico, Colorado, and Wyoming. This land was still part of Mexico. Mexico had fought its own war, for independence from Spain, in 1821. Mexico had won, but it was now too weak to control its territory. There had been border disputes between Mexico and the United States for several years. On April 23, 1846, the United States declared war.

Abe Lincoln, like other Whigs, believed the president was acting rashly. Lincoln vigorously declared to the House that "the war with Mexico was unnecessarily and unconstitutionally commenced by the President."

But many legislators disagreed. They talked on and on about the need of the country to expand, and about the brave soldiers who were fighting and dying for "manifest destiny."

Lincoln grew bored to tears at hearing these empty speeches. After listening to one speaker, he complained, "I never saw so many words compressed into so small an idea." Still, he voted to supply U.S. troops in Mexico with arms and other necessities. Since the president had gotten them into trouble, he reasoned, it would not be right to leave the men stranded.

By 1848, the war was over. The United States had won, and the contested territories became part of the country. It was to be an important event for many reasons. The major debates of the next decade would be about slavery. The most important issue at hand was whether slavery would be permitted in these new lands.

For the time being, this matter did not concern Lincoln directly. At the end of his two-year term in Congress, he did not seek reelection, but instead returned to Springfield. There, William Herndon had kept the law practice running smoothly. Abe returned to his family and to the life of a country lawyer.

He traveled a great deal, bouncing along the rutted roads in a little buggy, meeting citizens all over the state, and handling cases large and small, many of which he argued before the Supreme

Court of Illinois. Some involved important issues, like the taxing of the railroad. Others were more private affairs.

In one case, he defended a man named Duff Armstrong in a murder trial. A witness claimed that, although it was night, he saw Armstrong striking the victim in the moonlight. Lincoln used an almanac to prove that there was no moon shining that night. He won the case.

When he was home in Springfield, he spent his free time with his family. Robert and Edward were growing fast, and Mary was happier than she had ever been. She and her husband had a nice home, and she was able to afford a housekeeper to help with the boys. But it was not the luxurious life Mary had known as a girl in Kentucky, when servants did all the work. Now she did her own cooking. She baked hams and cooked chickens and woodchucks. She also made her own calf's foot jelly, canned her own blackberry jam, and baked lots of cakes and cookies.

The family lived in a five-room house at the corner of Eighth and Jackson streets. On the door was a gold nameplate that said simply "A. Lincoln." It was the first home they owned. Abe had paid $1,500 for it. It was not in the fashionable section of Springfield, called Aristocrat's Hill, and this pleased Abe. His political opponents had been accusing him lately of being uppity and "high born." Most folks knew that, in fact, Abe Lincoln had been born in a log cabin. Still, he didn't want to appear too stylish.

Robert and Eddie liked it when their father was home. They would go for long walks together, the tall man loping down the street with one of the boys bouncing on his shoulders and the other running beside him. They would both chatter at the same time, fighting for their father's attention. Once a neighbor passed the threesome and saw the boys clawing at each other while Abe tried to keep them apart.

"What's wrong?" the man asked.

Abe chuckled. "Just what's the matter with the whole world," he said. "I've got three walnuts and each wants two."

Lincoln's happy family life was soon destroyed, however. Young Eddie had been a sickly boy from birth. At age four he fell ill with tuberculosis, which in those days was called consumption. It was then the most common cause of death. For nearly two months, the boy suffered fever and terrible coughing fits. Finally, in February 1850, he died.

Mary Lincoln reacted more with anger than sadness. She felt outraged that her son had been taken from her. Her husband tried to comfort her while he dealt with the sadness in his own heart. The Lincoln household would never be quite as cheerful as before.

6

A FEVER PITCH

"As a nation, we began by declaring that 'all men are created equal.' We now practically read it 'all men are created equal, except negroes.'"
ABRAHAM LINCOLN, IN A LETTER
TO JOSHUA SPEED

By the time the Mexican War ended, huge new parcels of land were added to the Union. This area included what are now the states of New Mexico, Arizona, Colorado, Utah, Nevada, and California. The land-hungry Americans now had a much vaster territory to spread out across. To help pioneers to get to the new lands, the railroad became extremely important. Tracks were laid at a furious pace throughout the 1840s and 1850s. The country was on the move.

Back in 1820 the nation had made a similar move westward, into the wilderness lands of Illinois, Indiana, Ohio, Minnesota, Missouri, Kentucky, and Tennessee. At that time the new territories fueled the biggest battle in the young nation's history. The question had been: Should the new lands be open to slavery or not? It was decided in the Missouri Compromise, which drew a line at Missouri's southern border (36 degrees and 30 minutes latitude). All lands in the new areas that were north of the line (except Missouri itself) would be free of slavery when they became territories. Those to the south could have slavery if they chose to. This arrangement had kept the balance of power equal in the U.S. Senate. There were 11 free states and 11 slave states in 1819, before the Missouri Compromise. In 1821, there were 12 free states and 12 slave states, as well as one free and one slave territory. The two groups continued to have an equal number of senators. Neither side wanted the other to have an advantage.

In 1850 the same debate raged, this time even more heatedly. Once again the balance of power was threatened. If all the new lands became free states, the Southern senators would be outvoted in the future.

Another factor in the debate was the rise in technology. Back in 1820, the different parts of the country were much more isolated. In those simpler times, the United States was a vast collection of towns and counties that had little to do with one another. Most folks did not know or care much about what went on in the next county, let alone the next state. But by 1850 the march of technology had brought the various parts of the nation into closer contact. With railroads, steamboats, and telegraph lines connecting them, people couldn't help but take an interest in distant events. More and more often, those events would have an affect on them.

This meant that people in the three major sections of the country—the North, the West, and the South—were sitting up and taking notice of what people in the other parts were thinking and doing. Farmers in Massachusetts saw that their products were not being bought, and they realized it was because the vast farms in the West were producing more grains and vegetables that were of higher quality. For their part, the westerners were aware that Northerners thought of them as uncivilized rowdies.

Another source of tension in these difficult times was the immigrants who arrived in droves during the 1840s. Most of these were Irish and Germans who had fled poverty and political upheaval in their countries. They believed what they had heard about America: that it was the land of opportunity, where anyone willing to work hard and be honest could earn a good living.

But the masses of new citizens overwhelmed the Americans of Boston, New York, Philadelphia, and other cities and towns of the Northeast. Many of the newcomers did not understand English, and the established citizens worried that they would take their jobs.

The immigrant tide created a strange new political party. The members of this party were committed to the simple ways and simple life of the past. When outsiders asked what their party stood for, they replied simply, "I know nothing," for they were committed to keeping their organization a secret. They came to be known as the Know-Nothing party. In truth, they had a very definite position. The Know-Nothings were committed to defeat immigrant groups in elections and to support all "native" Americans. Many were anti-Catholic as well. Their battle cry was "Americans must rule America!"

The group soon became popular throughout the country. When Abraham Lincoln heard what they stood for, he scratched his head in confusion. He did not understand this talk of "native" Americans. As far as he knew, he said, the American Indians were the true native Americans. "We pushed them from their homes," he declared, "and now turn on others not fortunate enough to come over so early as we or our forefathers."

Lincoln wrote to his old friend Joshua Speed, saying: "Our progress in degeneracy appears to me to be pretty rapid. As a nation, we began by declaring that *'all men are created equal.'* We now practically read it 'all men are created equal, *except negroes.'* When the Know-Nothings get control, it will read 'all men are created equal, except negroes, *and foreigners, and Catholics.'*"

The Know-Nothings allied themselves with the Democratic party. The Democrats at the time found themselves trying to deal with another problem that threatened the nation, one that especially concerned the South: slavery. In 1820, Southerners had been worried about Northerners trying to stop the spread of slavery into new territories. Now it was happening all over again. Back then the Northerners were content to draw a line and let the Southerners do whatever they wanted south of it. Now, however, there were reasons for being concerned.

Now Southern Democrats insisted more firmly than ever that slavery was necessary. Many even wrote books and pamphlets arguing that slavery was morally right. They quoted the Bible to back up their claims.

In Congress, some of the men who had helped draft the Missouri Compromise believed it was still possible to reach an agreement that would partially satisfy everyone. Henry Clay and Daniel Webster worked hard to push the Compromise of 1850 through the Senate. As one result of this compromise, California was to be admitted as a free state, but voters in the other territories would be allowed to decide the slavery issue for themselves. Another part of the agreement stated that slavery would continue to be legal in the District of Columbia, but that the slave trade there would be illegal. And New Mexico was to get a part of Texas's land.

The "ayes" echoed around the Senate chamber. The bills were passed. But it was soon evident that the agreement pleased no one. Southerners were angry that California was to be a free state. Northerners who were against the spread of slavery were enraged that voters in future states in the West could possibly spread slavery further.

By 1854 another great chunk of the continent was ready to be divided into territories. The land in question included all of what are now the states of Kansas, Nebraska, North Dakota, and South Dakota, as well as parts of Montana and Wyoming.

At this, the debate rose to fever pitch. The South was up in arms. Southern legislators had only to look at a map to see that they were doomed. Most of the land in the new territories lay north of the 36° 30′ line. The South already had far fewer votes in the House of Representatives than the North, since it had a smaller population. Now the Southerners saw that when these territories were broken up into states most would be Northern free states. The Northerners would then control the Senate as well. In the Senate, each state is represented by two senators, no matter what its population. If this happened, the Senate would be able to outlaw slavery everywhere in the United States. This threatened the Southern way of life.

The South was determined to keep an even balance in the Senate, but nobody knew how it could be done. At this crucial moment, a fiery young Democratic senator from Illinois named

Stephen Douglas stood up on the floor of the chamber and asked permission to speak. Douglas had been a longtime foe of Abraham Lincoln, in more ways than one. The two had clashed over political issues many times in Illinois, and Douglas was also the man who had begun courting Mary Todd while she and Abe were engaged.

Douglas was a small, pudgy man with an enormous head and aloof, noble bearing. He now stood before the Senate and offered what he thought was an ingenious compromise. The vast area under consideration should be admitted to the Union as two territories, called Kansas and Nebraska, and in both of these the question of slavery should be left up the citizens to decide. The settlers in each territory would be free to "vote slavery up or down," as Douglas said. Douglas was not concerned with the moral right or wrong of slavery. He was more interested in the railroad reaching westward, and he knew that unless a compromise could be found the Southern senators would block it.

Douglas was a masterful politician. He forced his bill through the House and the Senate. It came to be known as the Kansas-Nebraska Act of 1854.

Around the country, a political explosion went off. Many Northerners had cared little about slavery up until this time. They saw it as an outdated institution that would eventually die out. But at this, they suddenly became furious. The Kansas-Nebraska Act destroyed the agreement set up in the Missouri Compromise. That act had insured that the Northern territories would always be free. Now slavery might be extend north of the "36° 30′ line. Many people feared that slavery was growing rather than slowly dying.

Those who were opposed to slavery on moral grounds were called abolitionists because they wanted to abolish, or destroy, the institution of slavery. There had been abolitionists in the United States practically from the nation's birth, but they were a very small minority. Most whites considered them "extremist," because their position would change the country so radically. In the 1830s, William Lloyd Garrison had begun publishing a pro-abolition newspaper called the *Liberator.* It was dedicated to ending slavery immediately and in every part of the nation. Although it was

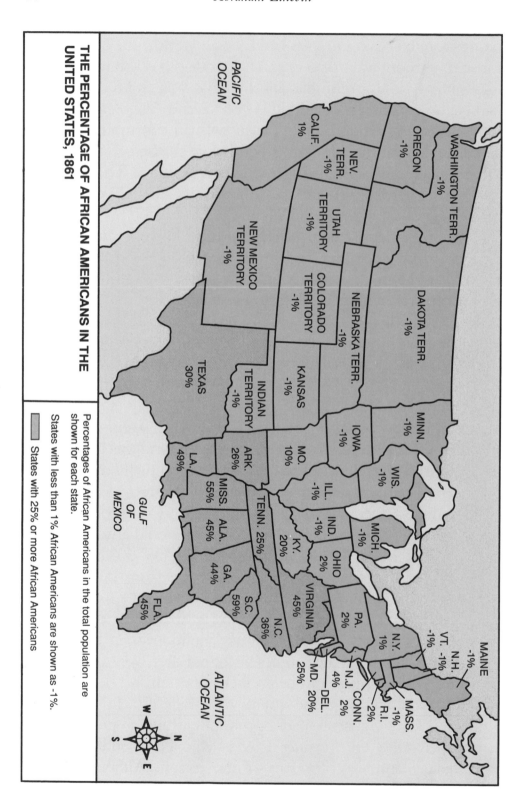

THE PERCENTAGE OF AFRICAN AMERICANS IN THE UNITED STATES, 1861

Percentages of African Americans in the total population are shown for each state.

States with less than 1% African Americans are shown as -1%.

States with 25% or more African Americans

PACIFIC OCEAN

WASHINGTON TERR. -1%

OREGON -1%

CALIF. 1%

NEV. TERR. -1%

UTAH TERRITORY -1%

NEW MEXICO TERRITORY -1%

DAKOTA TERR. -1%

NEBRASKA TERR. -1%

COLORADO TERRITORY -1%

TEXAS 30%

INDIAN TERRITORY -1%

KANSAS -1%

IOWA -1%

MINN. -1%

WIS. -1%

MO. 10%

ILL. -1%

IND. -1%

MICH. -1%

ARK. 26%

LA. 49%

MISS. 55%

ALA. 45%

TENN. 25%

KY. 20%

OHIO 2%

GA. 44%

FLA. 45%

S.C. 59%

N.C. 36%

VIRGINIA 45%

PA. 2%

N.Y. 1%

VT. -1%

N.H. -1%

MAINE -1%

MASS. -1%

R.I. 2%

CONN. 2%

N.J. 2%

DEL. 20%

MD. 25%

GULF OF MEXICO

ATLANTIC OCEAN

W N S E

published in the "free" city of Boston, Garrison was attacked by an angry mob. In Lincoln's home state of Illinois, Elijah Lovejoy had been killed for printing similar views. The vast majority of Americans, even in the North, were not ready to support complete freedom for blacks.

But now, in 1854, things had changed. Two very different groups of Northerners came together. The abolitionists, who wanted an end to slavery on moral grounds, and the larger group of Northern whites who were angered over the Kansas-Nebraska Act suddenly found themselves on the same side.

In Kansas itself, the act had bloody consequences. Pro-slavery and anti-slavery forces wrestled for control of the new state. Fights broke out as angry citizens clashed. More than 200 people died, and many more were injured.

In the turmoil following the passage of the Kansas-Nebraska Act, the Whig party was split in two. Unable to take a unified stand on slavery, the party quickly died out. Those who supported slavery, or believed it should be left to individual states to decide, joined the Democratic party. Most of those who called for an end to slavery joined with abolitionists and other Northerners in forming a new political party, called the Republicans. Now there was a new division in American politics. The most powerful issue was slavery, and the two sides were forming, one in the North and one in the South.

THE DOUGLAS DEBATES

> "'A house divided against itself cannot stand.' I
> believe this government cannot endure,
> permanently half *slave* and half *free*."
>
> LINCOLN, ACCEPTING THE REPUBLICAN
NOMINATION FOR THE SENATE, 1858

be Lincoln had been retired from politics for six years, practicing law in Illinois with his partner, William Herndon. The events of 1854, however, affected him as much as they did the rest of the nation. The shock, he said, echoing the words of President Jefferson, was like "the sound of a fire-bell in the night."

His chance to do something would come, of all places, at a state fair. The Lincoln family went to the fair to buy household goods and watch the judging of hogs and cattle. Abe and Mary had had two more sons by this time: William, age four, and Thomas, who was a baby less than a year old. The family had a pleasant morning amid the excitement of the booths and contests. Everyone was pleased when Mary's sister, Ann, won a prize for embroidery.

Abe made it a point to be on hand to listen to a speech to be given that afternoon by Senator Stephen Douglas. Inside the Springfield statehouse, Douglas defended his Kansas–Nebraska Act, his deep voice echoing through the chamber. It was only right, he argued, for the people of a state or territory to decide for themselves whether to permit slavery. Citizens of other states had no right to interfere with their business.

Abe Lincoln was enraged. He had been out of national politics for some time but had followed events closely. He had also done a

58

great deal of thinking about the slavery issue. His partner, William Herndon, was a devout abolitionist who had argued with him many times that slavery was ethically wrong. Herndon had given him abolitionist books and papers to read, such as the *Emancipator* and the *Anti-Slavery Standard*. But Lincoln had always been slow and deliberate in his thinking. His mind worked carefully and steadily on problems. Besides, he knew a sudden decision on this issue could tear the country apart.

Now, listening to Douglas, Lincoln made an unusually quick decision. The opposition was due to make a response to Douglas's speech the next day. Lincoln got himself selected as the speaker.

A huge crowd gathered in the chamber the next day to hear what was sure to be a fiery response. Everyone knew of the long rivalry between Douglas and Lincoln. Now, at this tense moment of history, Lincoln was stepping forward to take on his old foe.

Lincoln's speech was masterful. Afterwards Herndon wrote an editorial in the newspaper, saying:

"The anti-Nebraska speech of Mr. Lincoln was the profoundest in our opinion that he has made in his whole life.... He quivered with emotion.... He was most successful, and the house approved the glorious triumph of truth by loud and continued huzzas [cheers]. Women waved their white handkerchiefs in token of woman's silent but heartfelt assent."

"Wherever slavery is, it has been first introduced without law," Lincoln proclaimed. Then he wondered aloud, "What natural right requires Kansas and Nebraska to be open to slavery? Is not slavery universally granted to be a gross outrage on the law of nature?"

Still, Lincoln was not prepared to go as far as his law partner. He asked, what should be done with the slaves? "Free them, and make them, politically and socially, our equals? My own feelings will not admit of this, and if mine would, we well know that those of the great mass of white people will not. Whether this feeling accords with justice and sound judgment, is not the sole question, if indeed, it is any part of it."

By this, Lincoln meant that although he believed slavery was a moral outrage, he did not think it was possible for slaves to be made free and become equal with whites in all ways. He still believed that the best hope for the nation was to go back to the old Missouri Compromise, which would allow the South to have slavery.

Yet Lincoln's speech electrified the citizens of Illinois. And it electrified him, too. He now made up his mind to enter politics again. He left the rapidly dying Whig party (he said that he was now "unwhigged"), and joined the newly formed Republicans.

Lincoln lost his bid to become a U.S. senator in 1855, but he remained hopeful. By the middle of 1856, he was an important Republican known for his ability to state, clearly and logically, the case against the "Kansas-Nebraska" Democrats. In May, Lincoln addressed the first Illinois Republican state convention. The text of the speech is now lost, which is unfortunate because Herndon later said it was the greatest speech of Lincoln's life. "His speech was full of fire and energy and force," Herndon wrote, "...it was justice, equity, truth, and right set ablaze by the divine fires of a soul maddened by the wrong."

A newspaper said that after the speech "the audience sprang to their feet, and cheer after cheer told how deeply their hearts had been touched, and their souls warmed up to a generous enthusiasm."

From that day onward, Abraham Lincoln was looked upon by Illinois Republicans as their greatest hope.

The nation was dividing over the Kansas-Nebraska Act. In 1856 the Democratic party formally endorsed the act at its presidential convention. The Democrats nominated a moderate from Pennsylvania, James Buchanan, as their candidate.

The Republicans held their first convention in Philadelphia. They chose John C. Frémont, a brash soldier and explorer who had since become a U.S. senator, as their candidate for president. When it came time to select a vice presidential candidate, the voting was 259 for William Dayton, a former senator, and 110 for an Illinois man named Lincoln.

Not many of the delegates had heard Lincoln speak, but news of his forcefulness and cool reasoning ability had traveled quickly. He came in second in the voting without even knowing he was in the running. When he heard about it later, he joked that it must have been "some other Lincoln." But indeed, the new party now recognized Abraham Lincoln of Illinois as one of its leaders.

Lincoln campaigned hard for the Republicans. He crisscrossed Illinois speaking on behalf of Republican candidates and debating with Democrats. In one speech, he showed that he understood very clearly what the future would bring if the two sides could not come to agreement. The Democrats had begun arguing that the Republicans wanted to split the country in two. Now Lincoln cried:

"Who are the disunionists, you or we? We, the majority, would not strive to dissolve the Union. And if any attempt is made it must be by you. . . . But the Union, in any event, won't be dissolved. We don't want to dissolve it, and if you attempt it, we won't let you!"

The Republicans lost their first presidential election. James Buchanan was elected president, and he entered office with the nation more divided than it had ever been in the 70 years since Hamilton, Madison, and the other forefathers had signed the U.S. Constitution.

The next year the argument over slavery grew even louder. The United States Supreme Court heard a case brought by a black man named Dred Scott. Scott had been a slave in Missouri. Later he and his master moved to Illinois, which was a free state, and then to the northern part of the Louisiana Territory (now Minnesota). That part of the territory had been made free by the Missouri Compromise of 1820. Scott's lawyers argued that he should now be a free man because his master had brought him into free lands.

The Supreme Court, however, ruled that Scott must remain a slave. The Court's reasoning was the shocking thing. The justices said that Scott was not entitled to bring a case to court at all because he was a black man, and blacks could not be considered citizens of the United States.

Further, the Supreme Court held that the Missouri Compromise itself, in which Congress set the slavery boundary, was unconstitutional because the Congress had no right to make such a declaration. The Court ruled that slaves were property and citizens could not be denied their property without due process under the terms of the Fifth Amendment to the Constitution.

The *Dred Scott* decision shocked millions of Americans. It also shocked Congress. The decision meant that the whole matter of which states could be free and which were allowed to keep slavery was thrown open again. One of those most alarmed was Abraham Lincoln.

By 1858, Lincoln had become the best-known Republican in Illinois. In June, he easily won the party's nomination to become the Republican candidate for the Senate. The resolution said: "Resolved, That Abraham Lincoln is the first and only choice of the Republicans of Illinois for the United States Senate, as the successor of Stephen A. Douglas." After the resolution was read, the assembly erupted in applause.

That evening the House of Representatives was packed with Republicans who assembled to hear their candidate. It was a hot summer night, and the air in the chamber was thick. Abraham Lincoln, now nearly 50 years old, stood tall and gaunt before the convention. In his hand he held a speech that was to become one of the most legendary in American history.

"'A house divided against itself cannot stand,'" Lincoln thundered, using words from the Bible to describe the perilous situation the country faced. He went on:

> I believe this government cannot endure, permanently half *slave* and half *free*. I do not expect the Union to be *dissolved*—I do not expect the house to *fall*—but I *do* expect it will cease to be divided. It will become *all* one thing, or *all* the other. Either the *opponents* of slavery will arrest the further spread of it, and place it where the public mind shall rest in the belief that it is in course of ultimate extinction; or its *advocates* will push it forward, till it shall become alike lawful in *all* the States, *old* as well as *new*—*North* as well as *South*.

This was the clearest presentation of the slavery issue that had ever been made. Douglas's Kansas-Nebraska Act, Lincoln said, was really an attempt to "educate and mold public opinion... to not care whether slavery is voted down or voted up." And the Dred Scott decision was a clever, but desperate, attempt to find a logical, legal basis for the continuation of slavery. If the Republicans did not oppose it, he said, slavery would eventually spread.

Now the battle lines over the slavery issue were clearly drawn. Two great "armies' faced one another. And each side had its general: The Democrats had Senator Stephen Douglas, the nationally known author of the Kansas-Nebraska Act, and the Republicans had a tall, determined, forthright country lawyer named Abraham Lincoln. The whole state, and much of the country, focused on the battle between these two powerful spokesmen.

Over the next few weeks, the two candidates traveled around the state, speaking to different crowds on different days. Then, in July, Lincoln challenged Douglas to a series of debates. Douglas accepted. The most famous political battle in the history of the nation began.

When the first debate was held in Ottawa, Illinois, on August 21, it seemed as though the whole state felt the importance of the occasion. At sunrise a dense mass of people was descending on the city of Ottawa. "Teams, trains and processions poured in from every direction like an army with banners," the local newspaper reported. "National flags, mottoes and devices fluttered and stared from every street corner." By the time the two candidates were in place on the speaking stand in the center of town, 12,000 people jammed the public square.

The opponents were as different as two men could be. Douglas, who was known as the Little Giant, was small, round-faced, almost dainty looking. His hair was carefully combed back and his suit was neatly arranged. Lincoln stood six feet four inches tall, an awkward tower of a man. His hair was scattered; his clothing looked worn and wrinkled.

Douglas began the debate with a one-hour speech. In powerful language he accused Lincoln of being an abolitionist who refused to allow the citizens of the states the right to make their own decisions. He proudly stated that his own beliefs were those of the vast majority of Americans. "My principles are the same every-

THE GREAT DEBATES

The Illinois senate campaign of 1858 was one of the most legendary in United States history. Two fiery opponents squared off against one another in a heated series of debates that captured the spirit and tension of the times. The two men could not have been more different. Abe Lincoln was tall and ungainly, with a sad, peaceful expression. Senator Stephen Douglas was called the Little Giant. He was short and squat, dressed carefully and expensively, and had a determined gleam in his eye. The debates covered many topics, but slavery was the one that drew thousands of spectators to each debate. The two men argued about whether new states should have the right to allow slavery. But the underlying question, which Lincoln stressed at every opportunity, was the evil of the institution itself. He declared that the debate was "the eternal struggle between these two principles—right and wrong—throughout the world." The debates made Lincoln's name famous all over the country.

Ambitious Senator Stephen Douglas hoped a reelection in 1858 would launch him toward the presidency.

Lincoln was almost unknown outside Illinois before the debates.

where," he said. "I can proclaim them alike in the North, the South, the East, and the West." He was sure that most Americans agreed with his opinions. "Now, I do not believe that the Almighty ever intended the negro to be the equal of the white man," he told the crowd. "For thousands of years the negro has been a race upon the earth, and during all that time, in all latitudes and climates, wherever he has wandered or been taken, he has been inferior to the race which he has there met."

Lincoln stood when it was his turn to speak. He first answered Douglas's charges. He explained that he was not an abolitionist and accused Douglas of twisting the meaning of his past speeches. Douglas, he said, liked to play with words and so prove that a horse chestnut is the same thing as a chestnut horse.

Lincoln said he did not wish to abolish slavery. He knew the great majority of voters did not like the idea of abolition. Instead, he argued that slavery should be restricted to the original states of the south. Eventually, he said, it would die out. But Stephen Douglas's Kansas-Nebraska Act meant that slavery had a chance to gain strength in the country. "When he invites any people willing to have slavery, to establish it," Lincoln said of Douglas, "he is blowing out the moral lights around us. When he says he 'cares not whether slavery is voted down or voted up,'—that it is a sacred right of self-government—he is in my judgment penetrating the human soul and eradicating the light of the reason and the love of liberty in this American people."

At the end, the crowd cheered for both men. Lincoln was surrounded by his supporters. So was Douglas. There were six more debates all around the state. Douglas would arrive in town on the train in high style, in his own personal car. Lincoln would come in some time later on the regular coach, surrounded by squawking chickens, playing children, and poker-faced farmers. Douglas, the senator, would be greeted by the city fathers and escorted to his hotel. Lincoln would hitch a ride in a hay wagon.

At every stop the crowds gathered and swelled. People sensed that this fiery exchange was important to the whole country. Shorthand note-taking had recently been invented, and reporters could now jot down the words of the speakers almost as fast as they were uttered. Newspapers in the East carried blow-by-blow accounts of the debates, giving long descriptions of the well-known Senator Stephen Douglas and of his obscure challenger, Abraham Lincoln.

Throughout all the debates, Senator Douglas kept talking about the extension of slavery into new territories. "Popular sovereignty" was the term he used to refer to the rights of the citizens to decide for themselves whether to allow slavery in their state.

But Lincoln kept steering the discussion back to the moral wrong of slavery. "That is the real issue," he told the crowd at Alton, the site of the debate. "That is the issue that will continue in this country when these poor tongues of Judge Douglas and myself shall be silent. It is the eternal struggle between these two principles—right and wrong—throughout the world."

In the middle of October, with the debate in the town of Alton, the great debate series came to an end. It was now up to the voters of Illinois to make their choice.

On November 1, the day before the election, Lincoln was making a final appearance. It poured rain, and Lincoln and Henry Villard, a reporter, found themselves squatting in a box-car to escape getting wet. Villard asked if Lincoln thought he would make a good senator.

"I am convinced that I am good enough for it," Lincoln said as he squatted, his arms wrapped around his bony legs, "but, in spite of it all, I am saying to myself every day: 'It is too big a thing for you; you will never get it.' Mary insists, however, that I am going to be Senator and President of the United States, too."

Lincoln laughed at the idea of it. "Just think of such a sucker as me as President!" he roared to the reporter.

The next day the Illinois voters made their choice for senator. Lincoln received more votes than Douglas. But that did not mean he won the Senate seat. The winner would be chosen by the legislators, not the popular vote. And the Democrats had won the majority of the legislative seats. Therefore, Douglas was reelected.

Abe Lincoln felt sore inside when it was clear he had lost. He told friends that he was pleased that his cause got the attention of people across the nation. But he was also sad. He returned to his home at

Eighth and Jackson Streets in Springfield and spent two weeks alone with his family. Mary was just as pained by the loss as her husband. She was an ambitious woman. She was also worried about her family. She and Abe wondered what would come next. He had spent a year running for the Senate. Now their money was gone, and the future was uncertain.

As to how Abe Lincoln felt inside, he later described it by telling a story. "I felt like the boy that stumped his toe," he said. "It hurt too bad to laugh, and he was too big to cry."

PRESIDENT LINCOLN

"Abraham Lincoln of Illinois is selected as your
candidate for President of the United States!"

GEORGE ASHMUN, CHAIRMAN,
REPUBLICAN CONVENTION OF 1860

On the night of October 16, 1859, a band of 21 men moved silently through the forest outside Harpers Ferry, Virginia. All were armed. Their leader was a wild-eyed abolitionist named John Brown who three years earlier had lead an attack on a pro-slavery settlement in Kansas. Now their target was the federal arsenal, which is where the weapons were stored.

Working swiftly, the men took control of the arsenal. Brown wanted to use this remote spot as a base to which escaped slaves could run. Two days later, the U.S. cavalry attacked the arsenal. Brown and his men surrendered. Brown was tried for murder and treason, and later hanged.

This episode seemed to awaken the worst fears of Southerners. Newspapers all across the South were soon announcing that Northern abolitionists were descending on them, murdering honest slaveholders and establishing military camps. Of course, the rumors were untrue, but they added to the extreme tensions between the North and the South. Southerners did not know what lay ahead, but they began preparing for the worst.

Meanwhile, back in Illinois, Abraham Lincoln found that although he had lost, he was a very popular loser. The Lincoln-

John Brown's abolitionist uprising was one of many events that hastened the Civil War.

Douglas debates had spread his name all over the country. A wealthy traveler from Illinois, Jesse Fell, reported to Lincoln that people around the nation were saying to him, "Who is this man Lincoln, of your state?"

Fell sat down with Lincoln and began asking questions about his past. He wanted to know what kind of man Lincoln was. He told him that he believed Lincoln would make an excellent candidate for president.

Lincoln scoffed. Everyone knew that William Seward, senator from New York, was the natural choice for the Republican party. He was well known, powerful, and experienced. What chance would Lincoln have against him?

In fact, many Republican leaders were beginning to think Lincoln would have a good chance. Seward had made many enemies in his years in power. So had the other leading Republicans. The country was in turmoil. Many leaders believed the next election would be a turning point in its history, when the question of slavery would finally be settled. Some Republicans liked the idea of running the tall, forceful, homespun lawyer from the West as their candidate.

Still, Lincoln thought the idea was crazy. He politely told Fell he was not interested in running. He did, however, take a trip through several states, during which he made speeches about the great issues of the day. He summarized for these audiences his position on slavery. He met many influential Republicans. He also became friends with several German-American leaders. Most of the 1.3 million foreigners who had immigrated to the United States were Germans, and these new citizens were eager to vote. They liked Lincoln's views opposing the Know-Nothing positions.

In October a letter arrived at Lincoln and Herndon's law office. It was from an influential citizens' group in New York. They wanted Lincoln to speak to them. Lincoln asked Herndon for advice. Lincoln had spoken to many groups, but he was nervous about appearing in New York City. He still felt awkward about his backwoods origins. Would they ridicule him?

Herndon urged him to go, and he did. He appeared at the Cooper Institute in February 1860. In the audience were some of the most powerful men of the day, including newspaper editors William Cullen Bryant and Horace Greeley. Lincoln must have seemed an odd fellow to these Easterners. One man in the audience said that when Lincoln stood before them he was "so angular and awkward that I had, for an instant, a feeling of pity for so ungainly a man. His clothes were ill-fitting, badly wrinkled—as though they had been jammed carelessly into a small trunk."

When Lincoln began speaking, several in the crowd winced. All his life Lincoln kept his backwoods pronunciation of certain words. Now he began by saying "Mr. Cheerman" for "Mr. Chairman." In his speech he said "git" instead of "get" and "heered" instead of "heard." People in the audience, who were considering this man as their candidate, shook their heads. One man later told a reporter that his thoughts were: "Old fellow, you won't do; it's all very well for the wild West, but this will never go down in New York."

Then something strange began to happen. As the man in the audience later said, "I forgot his clothes, his personal appearance, his individual peculiarities. Presently, forgetting myself, I was on my feet with the rest, yelling like a wild Indian, cheering this wonderful man. In the close parts of his arguments, you could hear the gentle sizzling of the gas burners. When he reached a climax the thunders of applause were terrific."

Lincoln spoke about the need to keep slavery out of the western territories. He argued that the founding fathers understood that slavery would eventually die out, and in the 1770s and 1780s slavery was less important to the country. The invention of the cotton gin had changed everything, however. Slavery was a thriving business in the 1850s, and men like Lincoln believed that it must be severely limited or else it would grow instead of dying. He finished his speech with the words, "Let us have faith that right makes might, and in that faith, let us, to the end, dare to do our duty as we understand it."

"When I came out of the hall," said the man in the audience, "my face was glowing with excitement and my frame was all a-quiver; a friend, with eyes aglow, asked me what I thought of Abe Lincoln, the rail-splitter. I said, 'He's the greatest man since St. Paul.'"

Many other New Yorkers were just as impressed with the speech. The newspapers began calling him the "man of the people." Afterward, Lincoln made a trip to New England and spoke to many assemblies there. When he returned home, he found his Illinois friends making plans to run him against Seward for the Republican nomination. Now he did not object. For the first time, he believed he had a chance.

Around the country, word was spreading. The Lincoln-Douglas debates had been printed in book form and the book was selling well. Now stories of the man from the backwoods of Illinois began to circulate. Folks in small towns around the country talked about the man who had been born in a log cabin, had worked as a storekeeper, and had taught himself the law.

This same man seemed to understand the confusing problems the country faced, and could see the way to solving them. He was not a famous senator, but that was even better in a way. People liked the idea of a common man, a "man of the people," for president.

On May 16, 1860, the Republican convention began in Chicago. The delegates from around the country had to choose a presidential nominee and a party platform that would state their positions. The platform they finally decided on was bold and outspoken. They stated their belief that it was unlawful for slavery to be extended and said that "the opening of the slave trade would be a crime against humanity."

When it came to choose their leader, the Republican delegates argued, debated, and finally voted. There was a total of 465 votes; one man needed 233 to win. On the first ballot the total was: $173\frac{1}{2}$ votes for Seward, 102 for Lincoln. The voting went to a second ballot. Now it was $184\frac{1}{2}$ for Seward and 181 for Lincoln. Before the third ballot, Lincoln's supporters worked furiously behind the scenes to get lukewarm Seward men to change their minds. On the third ballot it was $231\frac{1}{2}$ for Lincoln to 180 for Seward. Lincoln was now only $1\frac{1}{2}$ votes short of winning the nomination.

At last, on the fourth ballot there was a dramatic shift of votes. In the final tally, 364 votes were cast for Lincoln. "Abraham Lincoln of Illinois is selected as your candidate for President of the United

States!" cried the chairman. Hannibal Hamlin of Maine was chosen as the vice presidential nominee.

The hall erupted in cheers. Celebrations went on long into the night. But Lincoln himself was not there. He had stayed at home in Springfield. As it happened, he was at the general store buying a few supplies for Mary when a crowd gathered and the news came that he had been nominated. Cheers went up and suddenly everyone wanted to shake hands with their neighbor.

Lincoln, an awkward smile spread across his face, shook every hand. Then he said, "My friends, I am glad to receive your congratulations, and as there is a little woman down on Eighth Street who will be glad to hear the news, you must excuse me until I inform her."

The Democratic convention did not go so smoothly. Democrats were bitterly split over the slavery question. Many agreed with Stephen Douglas that slavery was a "necessary evil," and that it should be up to new states and territories to decide for themselves whether to allow it. But many Southern Democrats supported John Breckinridge of Kentucky, who was the current vice president. These delegates did not agree with the "necessary evil" label. In their minds slavery was morally right. They fervently believed that slavery was both good for the nation and good for the blacks, who, they thought, would otherwise be unable to function in society. They hoped the new territories would all adopt slavery.

The Democratic convention in Baltimore finally chose Douglas as their nominee. Immediately, 11 Southern states split from the party in anger and nominated Breckinridge as their candidate. The party was in chaos.

Meanwhile, the Republicans were unified. Senator Seward came to Springfield to meet with Lincoln. He promised to do all he could to get the New York and New England vote for the Republicans.

Throughout the long, hot summer months, Lincoln stayed in Springfield meeting continuously with advisors to make clear his position on the issues. They discussed election strategies and held

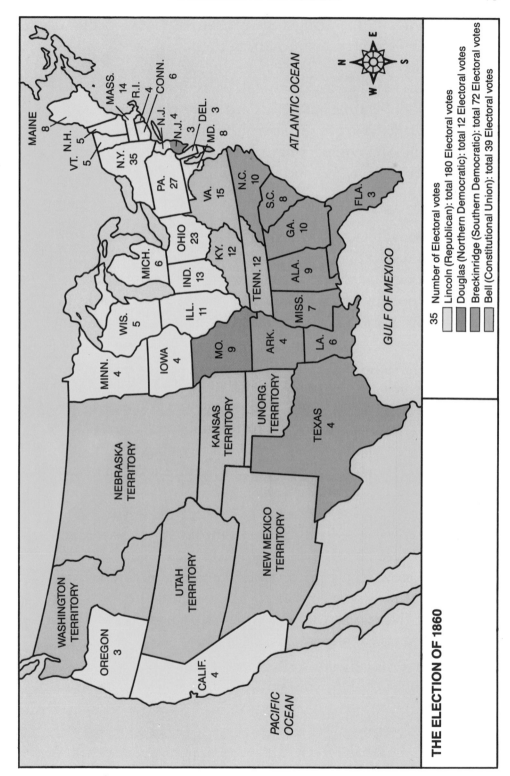

THE ELECTION OF 1860

35 Number of Electoral votes

Lincoln (Republican): total 180 Electoral votes

Douglas (Northern Democratic): total 12 Electoral votes

Breckinridge (Southern Democratic): total 72 Electoral votes

Bell (Constitutional Union): total 39 Electoral votes

MAINE 8

N.H. 5

VT. 5

MASS. 14

R.I. 4

CONN. 6

N.Y. 35

N.J. 4

N.J. 3

PA. 27

DEL. 3

MD. 8

VA. 15

N.C. 10

S.C. 8

GA. 10

FLA. 3

OHIO 23

KY. 12

TENN. 12

ALA. 9

MISS. 7

MICH. 6

IND. 13

ILL. 11

WIS. 5

IOWA 4

MINN. 4

MO. 9

ARK. 4

LA. 6

TEXAS 4

KANSAS TERRITORY

UNORG. TERRITORY

NEBRASKA TERRITORY

NEW MEXICO TERRITORY

UTAH TERRITORY

WASHINGTON TERRITORY

OREGON 3

CALIF. 4

ATLANTIC OCEAN

GULF OF MEXICO

PACIFIC OCEAN

long talks about the dangerous wedge that was being driven between the Northern and Southern states.

As the Republican candidate, Lincoln got letters from powerful politicians and businessmen from all parts of the country. He spent a good deal of his time answering his correspondence. In October there came a letter from an 11-year-old girl in New York named Grace Bedell. She wrote: "I have got 4 brother[s] and part of them will vote for you anyway and if you will let your whiskers grow I will try and get the rest of them to vote for you. You would look a great deal better for your face is so thin. All the ladies like whiskers and they would tease their husband[s] to vote for you and then you would be President."

Busy though he was, Lincoln wrote back to the girl. He asked her if she thought people would think it silly for him to grow a beard, since he had never worn one. Still, the girl's idea stayed in his mind.

On November 6, the nation chose its next president. Lincoln, along with half the town, was at the statehouse in Springfield. From time to time the results from a state would come in over the telegraph. They were strange, but not unexpected, results. Every Northern state but one (New Jersey) was voting for Lincoln, and every Southern state was voting against him. Never in history had there been such a definite division.

Late in the evening, the folks in Springfield learned that New York and Pennsylvania had favored Lincoln. That decided it. Abe Lincoln was president-elect. Springfield went mad with celebration. The crowds surged around the statehouse, chanting and singing. Lincoln joined in the celebration, then quietly left and went home. Mary was asleep in bed. He leaned over her, touched her shoulder, and whispered, "Mary, Mary, we are elected."

A House Divided

"My countrymen, one and all, think calmly and
well, upon this whole subject.... In your hands,
my dissatisfied fellow countrymen, and not in
mine, is the momentous issue of civil war."
PRESIDENT LINCOLN'S INAUGURAL ADDRESS

ix hundred miles southeast of the Lincoln home in
Springfield, the citizens of Charleston, South Carolina,
had heard the news also. Over the next few weeks, the
leaders of the most radical Southern state discussed their future. But
they all knew what they would do. The North had become
abolition–crazed, they told each other. Not a single South Caroli-
nian had voted for this man Lincoln. He was bound to destroy their
whole way of life. How could they possibly let him lead them?

Senator Robert Barnwell Rhett was the conscience of his state.
He put into words what many citizens believed: that South
Carolina must lead the South's break away from the Union. A
wild–eyed man who believed strongly in the good of the slave state,
Rhett talked, cajoled, and ranted until nearly every leader in the
state was in agreement with him. Then, on December 20, 1860, the
state leaders met in Charleston. There they formally seceded,
declaring that South Carolina was no longer a part of the United
States of America.

The word spread fast. Around the genteel city men whooped
and cheered. Marching bands played, and children squealed with
delight. Out across the state, in grubbly little hill towns and

riverside cities, the cries went up. The South was rising! Freedom
had come! Women wept for joy; men danced jigs in the street. For
white Southerners, the great day had arrived at last.

Like a wildfire spreading across the cotton plantations, the
exciting news swept the South. Over the next eight weeks, the six
major cotton states—Alabama, Georgia, Florida, Louisiana, Mississippi, and Texas—all declared their break with the United States
as well. The secession was real and growing.

On February 4, 1861, representatives of the seceded states met in
Montgomery, Alabama. Eighty-five years earlier, a roomful of
radicals had assembled in Philadelphia and declared their independence from England. Now these men—who saw themselves as
equally patriotic—boldly broke with their country and began a
new one, which they named the Confederate States of America.

They named a temporary president, Jefferson Davis. He had
served the United States valiantly as a colonel in the Mexican War.
As a U.S. senator from Mississippi, he had defended the interests of
Southern plantation owners and fought for the spread of slavery
into new territories. In 1853, Davis had served under President
Franklin Pierce as secretary of war. During this period he outfitted
the U.S. Army with a new, more accurate type of rifle. So Jefferson
Davis was responsible for the guns that would soon be aimed at his
new country.

In 1861, Davis took his place among the Southern leaders who
met in Richmond to form a new government. Because of his vast
military and political experience, the convention chose him as its
temporary president. As vice president they chose former senator
Alexander Stephens of Georgia. One month before, both men had
been serving as high elected officials in the United States Capitol.
Now they were leaders of a new enemy government.

After he had been made Confederate president, the stern Davis
said, "The South is determined to maintain her position, and make
all who oppose her smell Southern powder and feel Southern
steel."

In November the Confederacy would vote for a president to fill
a full six-year term. They would choose Davis.

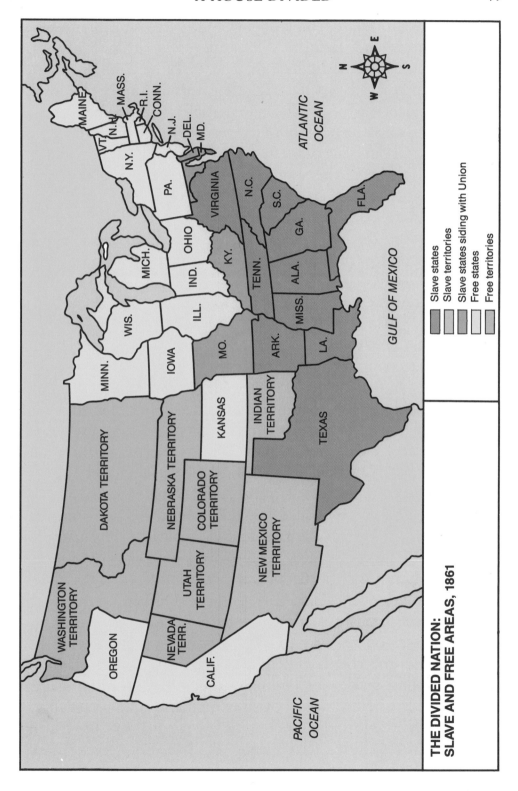

THE DIVIDED NATION:
SLAVE AND FREE AREAS, 1861

Slave states
Slave territories
Slave states siding with Union
Free states
Free territories

Meanwhile, further north, a train chugged across the prairie and through forests and farmland. It made stops in Indianapolis, Cincinnati, Columbus, Pittsburgh, and in New York State. At every stop it was greeted by a cheering throng of people, for it carried President-elect Lincoln and his wife, Mary. The crowds buzzed with excitement and questions. What would the new president do about slavery? What was going to happen to the country? Would he let the Southern states secede?

Lincoln spoke to each crowd in a serious, dignified manner. He wore a new suit, and in the weeks since the election he had grown a beard, following the advice of young Grace Bedell. On his head was a new hat, a present from well-wishers. (When Lincoln received the hat, he said to Mary, "Well, Mother, if nothing else comes out of this scrape, we are going to get some new clothes, are we not?")

Addressing the crowds, Lincoln sensed that for the first time in its history the country was coming apart, and just when he was to take charge. He told one crowd that "there has fallen upon me a task such as did not rest even upon the Father of his Country." He felt the immense responsibility already. Since he was an honest man, he no doubt wondered if he would be able to live up to it.

At the town of Westfield, New York, Lincoln said to the crowd, "I have a correspondent in this place, and if she is present I would like to see her." People looked around, wondering what famous woman from their town the president-elect meant. "Her name is Grace Bedell," Lincoln added. A shy young girl stepped forward. Lincoln took her by the hand and said, "You see, I let these whiskers grow for you, Grace." Then he kissed her.

It was an enormously exciting time for Abe Lincoln, the country lawyer. He was on his way to Washington, where he would be inaugurated as the country's 16th president. But he also had an ominous feeling inside, for he knew things were coming apart. Still, he had been filled with boyish excitement as he prepared to leave Springfield. He told Herndon, his law partner, that he wished to leave his name on the firm's sign. "If I live, I'm coming back sometime," he said, "and then we'll go right on practicing law as if nothing had ever happened."

He said "if I live" because he knew it was possible he would not survive. His election had brought about an enormous surge of hatred in many parts of the country. Threats of assassination reached his advisors all the time. The famous detective Allen Pinkerton was on hand to instruct the president-elect on security matters. Following his advice, Lincoln took a secret night train from Harrisburg through Baltimore—the center of assassination reports—to Washington. Instead of arriving in the capital city in presidential style, Lincoln was forced to sneak in like a criminal.

Mary, meanwhile, came the next day on the regularly scheduled train. In Baltimore, an angry crowd hurled insults, and some people even dashed through the train trying to find the man they called "the bloody Republican." But Abe was already in Washington.

On March 4, 1861, Abraham Lincoln was inaugurated as president. As he rose before the assembled dignitaries to give his inaugural address, he took off his new top hat, but he could not find a place to put it. Stephen Douglas, his old foe, whose own fame had brought Lincoln to popularity, was seated behind him. Douglas took the hat and, chuckling, whispered to Mary, "If I can't be president, I can at least hold his hat."

The address was a firm, even-handed statement of Lincoln's views of the crisis. He declared that "no state, upon its own mere motion, can lawfully get out of the Union." "I therefore consider," he went on, "that, in view of the Constitution and the laws, the

Lincoln was inaugurated in front of the unfinished Capitol building.

Union is unbroken; and, to the extent of my ability, I shall take care, as the Constitution itself expressly enjoins upon me, that the laws of the Union be faithfully executed in all the States."

He did not, however, call for war. "In doing this there needs to be no bloodshed or violence," he said, "and there shall be none, unless it be forced upon the national authority."

He then stated plainly the differences between North and South: "One section of our country believes slavery is right, and ought to be extended, while the other believes it is wrong, and ought not to be extended. That is the only substantial dispute...."

Finally, he begged the nation not to rush into war: "My countrymen, one and all, think calmly and well, upon this whole subject. Nothing valuable can be lost by taking time.... In your hands, my dissatisfied fellow countrymen, and not in mine, is the momentous issue of civil war."

But the issue was already decided. The Confederate government was already set up and operating even before Lincoln was sworn in. President Jefferson Davis and his quickly assembled cabinet (the people who would advise him during his term in office) were preparing for the worst.

The new Confederate government declared that it would stand for the principles of the U.S. Constitution, especially the protection of property and individual rights. The Southern leaders felt the federal government had abandoned these. The new Confederate constitution upheld slavery in the new nation and in any territories it might add. The Confederate leaders hoped European powers would soon aid them, but the Europeans did not like the South's strong support for slavery. Therefore, the Confederate constitution made it illegal to import slaves from abroad.

The constitution also protected the rights of individual states over the national government. States' rights were, after all, the reason the War Between the States was coming: the Southern states believed they had the lawful right to secede from the Union.

Southern men and boys were signing up for military service. Bands of unprepared men and boys were hastily drilled by the many army officers who had abandoned the United States and fled to their native states in the South. It was all very messy and confused, but the South was indeed preparing for war.

The atmosphere in South Carolina, the most enthusiastic Confederate state, was festive. Everyone felt a great surge of Southern pride at seeing their boys parading around in military drill. But one thing broke in on their pleasure. On an island in Charleston Harbor sat a squat stone building called Fort Sumter. It was a United States fort, and the Union flag flew over its battlements. The flag and the federal troops infuriated the people of Charleston. After all, the Confederacy was now a sovereign nation. It would not accept the presence of a foreign fort on its soil.

Confederate troops began taking position outside the fort. As weeks passed, more and more arrived, until the harbor had a dense throng of soldiers. The South wanted the 70 Union soldiers inside to get off their soil, but the soldiers were under orders to hold the fort.

Suddenly, just after his inauguration, President Lincoln had a crisis on his hands. Should he attack the Southerners with fresh troops? He quickly decided not to: that would be a declaration of war, and he was not going to be the one to begin the conflict. But he could not simply let his men be starved out of the fort. Therefore, President Lincoln's first major action was to inform Jefferson Davis that he was sending food and supplies to the Union men in Fort Sumter. He was not committing a hostile act.

President Davis responded quickly. If the men inside were stocked with provisions, they might stay forever. He ordered his men to open fire on the fort. For 34 hours the skies of Charleston were aglow with artillery fire. Bombs sailed into Fort Sumter, rocking the walls. In the end, Major Robert Anderson, commander of the fort, surrendered. His men evacuated. The Southerners whooped and celebrated. This business of war was still new to them. They were friendly with their prisoners. The were not used to the idea of capturing their former countrymen. Then they let the Union men go. The Union troops boarded a boat in the harbor and steamed northward. Fort Sumter was now in the hands of the Confederate troops. The Civil War had begun.

The nation was now formally split in two, and the two sides were in combat. But President Lincoln had other problems to deal with before he could get around to fighting a war. His first task after his election was to select his cabinet. He surprised everyone by choosing several of his former opponents to serve with him. Lincoln made William Seward, the experienced politician whom he had beaten at the Republican convention, his secretary of state. He chose another former opponent, Salmon P. Chase, as secretary of the treasury.

Each of these men had his own ideas about the presidency, and each believed that Lincoln, the backwoods lawyer, was too raw and untried to deal with the overwhelming crisis at hand. Seward sent the president a note one month into Lincoln's term that sounded more like a warning to a child than a suggestion for his boss. Seward complained that the administration was "yet without a policy, either domestic or foreign."

He was angry about rumors that France and Spain had been helping the South. He told Lincoln that he must demand explanations from those two countries, and "if satisfactory explanations are not received from France and Spain, I would convene Congress and declare war on them."

Lincoln immediately sent a reply to Seward. He firmly told his secretary of state that he, Lincoln, would decide such matters. If something must be done, he said, "I must do it." Then he shook his head and muttered to an assistant, "One war at a time."

On April 15, 1861, two days after Fort Sumter fell, the president issued a call for 75,000 troops to serve their country. These were temporary troops, to serve for only three months. Lincoln believed it was a minor rebellion he was dealing with, one that would be put down within a short time. With these troops, he hoped to rescue other forts in the South that had been taken by Confederate soldiers.

Lincoln had taken the decisive step. This was what many of the other Southern states had been waiting for. Two days after the call for troops, Virginia withdrew from the Union. Tennessee, Arkansas, and North Carolina soon followed. Virginia was the North's main concern. It lay just across the Potomac River from

Washington. President Lincoln could see its green countryside from his second-floor White House office.

With this land now part of the Confederacy, the United States army feared that Washington would be attacked. Union troops were sent south to defend the capital. However, Maryland, a slave state and one of the border states that did not approve of the war, lay in their path. A Maryland delegation told the president that 75,000 Maryland citizens were willing to block the way of the troops.

Lincoln knew when to stand firm. "I presume that you have room in Maryland for 75,000 graves," he said grimly. Federal troops took command of the city of Baltimore. The citizens made no more trouble.

Even after this, Lincoln found it difficult to wage a war. The United States Army had not fought since the Mexican War, and there were only a few old-timers around with battle experience. The state governments had control over the troops in their states, so the president had to ask their permission to use them. Each governor had his own ideas about the best way to deal with the threat.

Also, as in the South, the Union had very few trained soldiers. Following Lincoln's call, training grounds were set up all across the North, and officers went to work drilling raw recruits. The inexperienced farm boys that made up the units had no idea what they were getting themselves in for. To them it was all still a glorious party. Training to march in straight lines, to follow commands, prancing about with rifles and bayonets: it seemed like fun to them. They had never experienced the horrors of war. The generals were worried what would happen when they did.

Lincoln had problems even with his generals. The army was inefficiently organized at that time. Many men had risen to the rank of general through friends and associates, not talent and drive. One general complained that some of the brigadier-generals in the army were "entirely ignorant of their duties and unfit for any command."

Still, Abraham Lincoln hoped for a quick end to the conflict. He had good reasons for hoping so. The North was vastly superior to the South in many ways. For one thing, the population of the

North was double that of the South. There were about 18 million citizens in the Union, and 9 million in the Confederacy. Almost 40 percent of these Southerners were slaves, the vast majority of whom would not be sent into battle until very late in the war.

Another Northern advantage was industry. Most of the nation's factories were in the North. These could be set to work to turn out all the guns, ammunition, and other supplies that the Union soldiers needed. Also, to much of the world the North seemed to be fighting for freedom and equality, while the South was fighting to preserve the barbarity of slavery.

But the South had its advantages, too, and President Lincoln may have overlooked these in the early days of the war. For one thing, the war was being fought in the South. This meant that the Southerners would know the terrain better. Also, the Confederacy would be fighting a defensive war, which needed fewer men. It takes many more men to attack a position that it takes to defend it. And the South only had to survive, while the North had to conquer a vast territory.

Further, the South's leaders were hoping that some European nation would come to their aid. That could tilt the balance in their favor. Jefferson Davis and his associates hoped at least to hold their own until Northerners began to demand peace. There were already many Northerners crying out at the idea of "brother fighting brother." If the South could hold out until 1864, these Northerners might defeat Lincoln in the next election.

Another advantage for the South was its civic spirit. The Northerners joining the battle had national pride in their hearts, but it was not easy to see what they were fighting for. The Southern boy in the trenches knew that he was fighting to save his home and his traditions.

In his desire to win quickly, Lincoln ordered the U.S. Navy to blockade the Southern ports along the Atlantic. The blockade would prevent the South from receiving or shipping goods and supplies by sea. This was a good idea, but it was also one of many tactical errors Lincoln made in the war. The word "blockade" is used when referring to a foreign nation. In using it, Lincoln

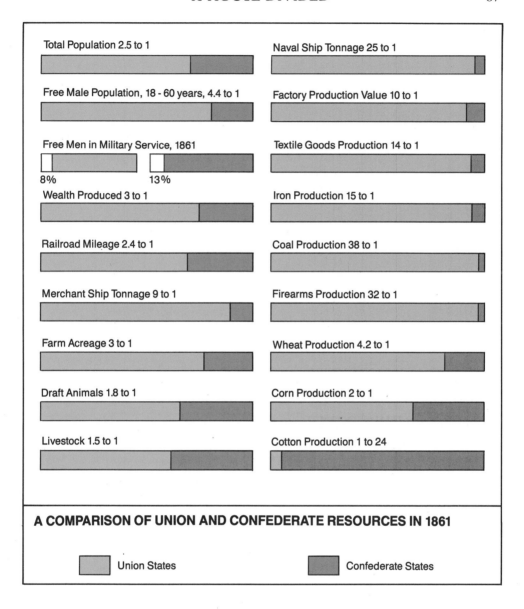

Total Population 2.5 to 1

Free Male Population, 18 - 60 years, 4.4 to 1

Free Men in Military Service, 1861
8%   13%

Wealth Produced 3 to 1

Railroad Mileage 2.4 to 1

Merchant Ship Tonnage 9 to 1

Farm Acreage 3 to 1

Draft Animals 1.8 to 1

Livestock 1.5 to 1

Naval Ship Tonnage 25 to 1

Factory Production Value 10 to 1

Textile Goods Production 14 to 1

Iron Production 15 to 1

Coal Production 38 to 1

Firearms Production 32 to 1

Wheat Production 4.2 to 1

Corn Production 2 to 1

Cotton Production 1 to 24

A COMPARISON OF UNION AND CONFEDERATE RESOURCES IN 1861

Union States   Confederate States

accidentally gave the Confederate State of America a kind of official recognition. This caused foreign governments to take notice. Some began to consider whether they should recognize the Confederacy as a separate nation.

Still, the blockade was a good plan, and as the war wore on it became very effective in cutting the South off from supplies. A major blockade in the West was the idea of Lincoln's first commanding general, Winfield Scott. Scott was a clever soldier, but he was very old by the time the Civil War broke out, and so ill that he could hardly stand up without the help of his lieutenants.

Scott was the only one of Lincoln's advisors who saw that the war would be a long one. He made a plan for blockading the Southern cities along the Mississippi River. This would take a long time, but it would slowly strangle the South.

Lincoln's other advisors scoffed at the plan. By the time it went into effect, they said, the war would be over. Soon Scott retired, the plan was dropped, and Lincoln looked around for another general. This proved difficult. Throughout much of the war, the president would search for one man with the strength and vision to lead the Union forces to victory. He would find that man, but not until much later.

THE SOUTH RISING

"There is no division among the people here.
There is but one mind, one heart, one
action.... What is seen in New Orleans pervades
the whole South. Never were people more
united and more determined."

MRS. R. L. HUNT OF NEW ORLEANS,
IN A LETTER TO HER BROTHER-IN-LAW,
U.S. SECRETARY OF THE TREASURY
SALMON P. CHASE

It was a hot summer day in the Manassas Plain near Centreville, Virginia. An air of excitement lingered over the hillside above Bull Run Creek. Society ladies from Washington, D.C.—20 miles away—sat on picnic blankets fancifully twirling their parasols. Men popped open bottles of champagne. People laughed and chattered. Then they quieted down and turned their attention to the show that was about to begin.

The "show" would become the first major battle of the Civil War. It was July 21, 1861. Union General Irvin McDowell had led his eager young recruits south from Washington into the Manassas Plain to strike terror into the hearts of the Confederates, or the "Rebels," as they had come to be called. He would crush the Rebel army here, and then, everyone in the North believed, the army would march gloriously on to Richmond, the Confederate capital. "Forward to Richmond! Onward to Richmond!" cried the *New York Tribune*. When McDowell's 35,000 troops took the city, people believed, the war would be over. It all seemed very simple.

But things did not work that smoothly. McDowell's troops were raw, inexperienced boys who had very little training. Armies of that time depended a great deal on drilling. There were no walkie-talkies, no way for officers to communicate quickly with one another once a battle was underway. Everything depended on the troops being well-trained. They had to learn how to stop, turn right, and about face while keeping the divisions together in tight, compact fighting machines. To enter battle without adequate training was to invite disaster.

Union scouts had been sent ahead. They reported that the Confederate troops were in position just across Bull Run. McDowell sent his first divisions, or smaller groups from the troops, straight at the enemy. The rest of the army swung slowly around to come in from the north in a big push that McDowell hoped would destroy the Rebel lines and send the soldiers running.

From the other side of the creek, Confederate General P.G.T. Beauregard watched the advancing Union army. It must have looked like a circus, for in these early days of the war there was no official uniform for either side, and the Union troops that now approached Bull Run were decked out in a bewildering variety of costumes. Everyone at the time admired Napoleon and the French army, so many soldiers wore uniforms imitating the bright colors of the French Zouaves. Some of the boys wore turbans on their heads and colorful scarves tied around their waists. Some divisions of Union troops were dressed all in gray, the color that the Confederate army would eventually choose, and some Confederate soldiers wore what would become Union blue.

Beauregard watched the colorful advance and heard the first whistling sounds of their artillery shells. He had been waiting for this moment. He was the man who had led the artillery attack on Fort Sumter. He was considered one of the South's greatest generals. Beauregard had only 20,000 troops, and they were no better trained than McDowell's men. Yet it would be an easier time for them. They would be in defensive position, not having to go through all the complex stops, starts, and turns of an attacking army.

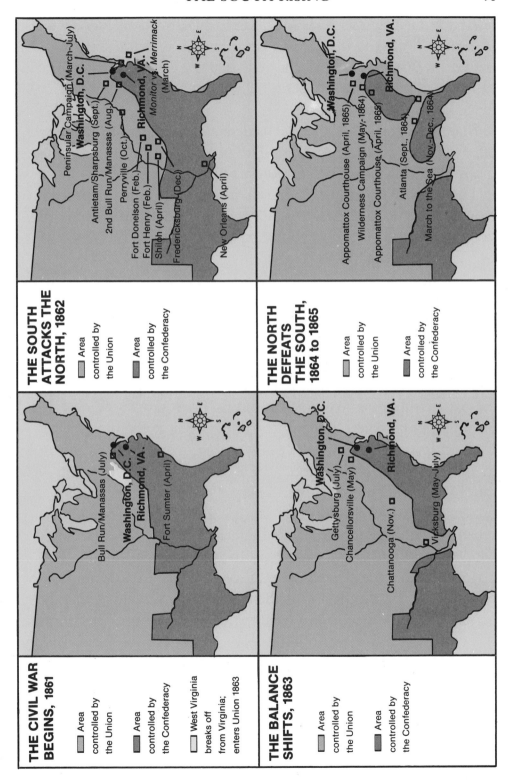

THE CIVIL WAR BEGINS, 1861

■ Area controlled by the Union

■ Area controlled by the Confederacy

□ West Virginia breaks off from Virginia; enters Union 1863

Washington, D.C.
Richmond, VA.
Bull Run/Manassas (July)
Fort Sumter (April)

THE SOUTH ATTACKS THE NORTH, 1862

■ Area controlled by the Union

■ Area controlled by the Confederacy

Peninsular Campaign (March–July)
Washington, D.C.
Richmond, VA.
Monitor vs. Merrimack (March)
Antietam/Sharpsburg (Sept.)
2nd Bull Run/Manassas (Aug.)
Perryville (Oct.)
Fort Donelson (Feb.)
Fort Henry (Feb.)
Shiloh (April)
Fredericksburg (Dec.)
New Orleans (April)

THE BALANCE SHIFTS, 1863

■ Area controlled by the Union

■ Area controlled by the Confederacy

Washington, D.C.
Richmond, VA.
Gettysburg (July)
Chancellorsville (May)
Chattanooga (Nov.)
Vicksburg (May–July)

THE NORTH DEFEATS THE SOUTH, 1864 to 1865

■ Area controlled by the Union

■ Area controlled by the Confederacy

Washington, D.C.
Richmond, VA.
Appomattox Courthouse (April, 1865)
Wilderness Campaign (May, 1864)
Appomattox Courthouse (April, 1865)
Atlanta (Sept., 1864)
March to the Sea (Nov.–Dec. 1864)

As the first artillery shells landed near the Confederate lines, Beauregard ordered his men to open fire. The battle was on. The crowd of Washingtonians cheered as if they were at the theater. Nobody in the nation realized yet how terrible real war was. They treated it as entertainment.

Major General Ambrose Burnside led his men in a frontal assault on the Confederate positions. The air filled with acrid smoke. Lines of Rebels fell. The crowd on the hill cheered.

The Union boys got confused in the complicated procedure required to reload their guns. Orders were delayed. Whole divisions never made it to the front lines of the battle. The Union force was falling apart.

Then disaster struck for the Union. Another Confederate army of about 10,000, led by General Joseph Johnston, was only 58 miles away. Johnston learned of the attack and put his troops on a train headed for Manassas Junction. They arrived just in time to help drive the Union soldiers into a panic.

Now the Washington citizens who had been picnicking above the battlefield began to look confused. They saw the Union lines breaking and soldiers starting to run . . . right at them!

Quickly people gathered their belongings and hurried out onto the road back to Washington. In a short time the retreating troops caught up with them. These troops, thinking they were being pursued, were wild-eyed with fright. The citizens, not knowing what was happening, were equally terrified. The bloodied soldiers tripped over high society ladies in their billowy skirts.

The Southerners, who were also confused, had stopped the pursuit. Their confusion cost them a major prize. Had they been better organized they might have marched straight to Washington. It would have been a crippling blow to the North. Instead, they had to be content with a sloppy, disordered victory. Still, it *was* a victory. Moreover, with the Battle of Bull Run, soldiers and civilians alike realized the difficulty of fighting a real war—and the horror.

In Washington, President Lincoln was shocked by the news of the defeat at Bull Run, in which nearly 3,000 men were killed or wounded. Newspapers called it a major disaster. Lincoln's own assistant secretary of war, Edwin Stanton, who had never believed that the crude lawyer from Illinois could lead the nation through the crisis, cried, "the imbecility of this Administration culminated in that catastrophe." Stanton called the loss at Bull Run a "national disgrace, never to be forgotten."

Suddenly the Union realized that fighting was a serious business. Congress now voted $500 million to support an all-out war effort and granted the president war powers.

One of the few men who knew all along that warfare required careful planning was Union General George McClellan. McClellan was an experienced soldier. He had fought in the Mexican War. He knew that victory in battle depended on many things that civilians never thought of, like keeping supply lines open and making sure that there was always a source of water nearby.

McClellan, assigned to territory farther west, had just won a small victory at the town of Philippi in western Virginia. Lincoln seized on this opportunity to put McClellan at the head of all the Union armies. McClellan was a popular general with the troops. He was a short, stocky young man, and he was considered brilliant. Because many people thought he looked like the great French general Napoleon, McClellan became known as "Little Napoleon."

Dressed in a crisp, neat uniform and riding a sleek horse, McClellan arrived in Washington and found the city in chaos. Soldiers, reeling drunkenly in the streets, feared that the Confederates would come sweeping down on the city. McClellan issued a sharp series of orders. Discipline returned overnight. In no time he had the loyalty of the whole army.

But McClellan also had problems. Unlike many others in the North, he understood the need for careful planning. The trouble was, he was too much of a planner. Days passed into weeks as Lincoln and his cabinet waited in vain for McClellan to carry out a major battle.

The citizens of the North were eager for victory. The cabinet pressed Lincoln, insisting that he force McClellan into action.

Edwin Stanton, who had now been named secretary of war, become more indignant than ever. One day someone reported to the president that Stanton had gone too far: in public he had called the president "a damned fool."

Lincoln knew when to be angry and when to laugh his way out of confrontations. He chuckled and said, "If Secretary Stanton called me a damned fool then I probably am one, for the secretary is usually right."

General McClellan (right of stump) was a brilliant strategist who lacked the guts to fight.

Nevertheless, Lincoln knew he would have to force McClellan into action soon, or replace him. As he lay awake at night in his bedroom in the White House, he must have wondered if there was a general in his army with the courage, daring, and experience to bring the Union to victory.

Secretary of War Edwin Stanton often disagreed with Lincoln's military decisions.

THE LINCOLN WHITE HOUSE

"Thousands of soldiers are guarding us. If there is safety in numbers, we have every reason to feel secure."

MARY TODD LINCOLN, IN A LETTER TO A FRIEND

The White House was a busy place during the war years. Cabinet officials, congressmen, important businessmen, generals, and secretaries streamed in and out of the building, all beseeching the president to see things their way. The building was also guarded by a cavalry contingent, as a last line of defense in case Washington were attacked. And there was the Lincoln family itself. The Lincolns were probably the most boisterous first family the White House had ever had.

To begin with, Mary Lincoln swept into Washington intent on living up to her new position. She had always been an ambitious woman, eager for her husband to become president long before he himself had thought of such a thing. Now she was determined to become an elegant and dignified first lady.

She got noticed quickly. One newspaper said of her, "She is more self-possessed than Lincoln, and has accommodated [adjusted] more readily than her taller half to the exalted station to which she has been so strangely advanced from the simple social life of... Illinois."

The first order of business for Mary Lincoln was the White House itself. To put it simply, the great home of the presidents was in awful shape. It was a dingy, creaky house that stifled with heat in the summertime and through which icy winds whipped in the winter. One government official said it reminded him of "an old and unsuccessful hotel." There was broken and tattered furniture, faded wallpaper, and a sad, neglected air about the whole place.

Mary Todd Lincoln was determined to turn the White House into a mansion worthy of European nobility.

Mary Lincoln went to work. She interviewed furniture makers, held long meetings with wallpaperers and drapers, and oversaw the decoration of the White House. The newspapers complained that the first lady was spending a fortune to beautify her home while the nation needed all its treasury reserved to fight the war. But Mary Lincoln was undaunted. She believed the president's home must be a grand, dignified place. Otherwise officials from the refined nations of Europe would be justified in thinking of the United States as a crude, barbarous newcomer.

The highlight of her social life at the White House came when Prince Napoleon, distant relative of Napoleon the conqueror, came to dinner. Everything was done in French style, and afterwards the newspapers expressed their pride at having a first lady who could speak French and knew how to entertain royalty.

While Mary was fixing up the White House and the president was busy conducting the Civil War, their two younger sons, Tad and Willie, enjoyed their new life very much. Their older brother, Robert, was away at Harvard College. The youngsters had the run of the White House, and every day there were new things to explore. Sometimes they would march with the soldiers on guard duty. Their father was always happy to see them. Visitors were often astonished when the two boys burst into the president's office and climbed into their father's lap while important war business was being discussed.

All in all, it was an exciting time for every member of the first family, except for the president himself. With each passing month his workday grew longer, and his face became more lined with worries. His secretary later said that the president would often get up well before six in the morning, have an egg and a cup of coffee, and head into his office. There, sitting at a large oak table before a white marble fireplace, he would begin his day. At first he tried to read every paper his secretaries and officials gave him to sign. Later he realized that was impossible, and he signed without reading, trusting his staff.

Throughout the morning the president would study war reports and discuss military strategy with close advisors. The news was gloomy. The country was in a full-scale civil war. Reports painted the nation red with bloodshed.

Twice a week the president held cabinet meetings. The spirited men whom Lincoln had chosen for his cabinet often argued loudly with one another and with the president over his conduct of the war. Lincoln liked the honesty.

In February 1862, the president, whose heart was filling with despair over the fate of his country, suffered a terrible loss. His 11-year-old son, Willie, and 8-year-old Tad were both struck with a strange fever. It is likely that it was typhoid fever, a disease caused by contaminated water. Tad fought off the disease and became well again, but Willie was always a weak child. He died on February 20.

The boy's funeral took place in the middle of the national crisis called the Civil War. One of Mary's friends who attended the funeral later wrote of the president: "And there sat the man, with a burden on the brain at which the world marvels—bent now with the load both at heart and brain—staggering under a blow like the taking from him of his child. His men of power sat around him—McClellan with a moist eye when he bowed to the prayer, as I could see from where I stood; and Chase and Seward, with their austere features at work; and senators, ambassadors and soldiers, all struggling with their tears."

Mary Lincoln was overwhelmed with grief following her son's death. She stormed about the White House in anger and frustration. Her doctors recommended rest. She went to bed and did not move for weeks, lying in a half-dead state. Something happened to her during that time from which she never recovered. When she finally left her bedroom, she no longer stormed and raged about the loss of her son, but quietly burned all of his things. Her husband feared for her health, but he let her be. He was trying to endure this painful period himself, and also trying to get the nation through the agony of the war.

FINDING A GENERAL

"It seems to me that McClellan has been
wandering around and has sort of got lost."

PRESIDENT LINCOLN

President Lincoln never had the support of all of the people in the North. There were many viewpoints expressed in newspapers and in Congress. Throughout the Civil War, thousands of people continued to disagree with the way it was being fought.

Disagreement turned into violence at times. On August 4, 1862, Lincoln called for 300,000 new recruits. Many states had to draft men into service, as there were not enough volunteers. Being forced into military service infuriated people who were against war. These antiwar groups attacked recruiting stations in several states during 1862 and 1863.

In New York City the draft led to riots. There, poor whites—mostly Irish immigrants—resented wealthier families who avoided the draft. (People were allowed to avoid military service by paying someone to enlist in their place.) These poor Northern whites felt that Abraham Lincoln was trying to increase their suffering by freeing the slaves of the South, who would then compete with them for the lowest-paying jobs. They started a riot that spread through the city, lasting four days and killing more than 100 people.

President Lincoln also faced the opposition of more organized groups. Many Northern Democrats opposed the war. They believed that the Confederacy ought to be allowed to split from the Union. Republicans gave them the nickname "Copperheads" because they believed that, like the copperhead snake, these Democrats represented a dangerous, lurking force.

As the war dragged on, the Copperheads became more and more vocal in their opposition to Lincoln's policies. They warned that Lincoln wanted to free the slaves, who would then stream North to overrun the cities. The Democrat-run newspapers asked, "Shall the Working Classes be Equalized with Negroes?"

And the newspapers took out their anger on President Lincoln. "By whom and when was Abraham Lincoln made dictator in this country?" asked the *New York Daily News.*

Such accusations increased when Lincoln suspended the writ of habeas corpus. This writ is a legal procedure for setting free someone who is jailed so that he or she may be brought before a judge. The U.S. Constitution says the writ may be suspended "when in cases of rebellion or invasion the public safety may require it." It may also be suspended when local officials may be involved in a plot to overthrow the government.

Lincoln suspended the writ with the latter reason in mind. In Maryland, where there were a great many Confederate allies, the Union army arrested John Merryman, a wealthy man suspected of aiding the Rebels. Merryman's lawyers asked Roger Taney, Chief Justice of the United States, for a writ of habeas corpus so that Merryman could be freed. Taney issued the writ, but the U.S. army refused to free Merryman because Lincoln had suspended the writ.

Many other treason suspects were also detained. In the newspapers, the Copperheads increased their attacks on Lincoln's leadership.

With the coming of spring in 1862, the president saw the first hopeful signs of the war. On March 8 and 9, the Confederate ironclad ship *Virginia* (formerly the Union ship *Merrimack),* which had been terrifying the Northern fleet in Norfolk harbor, met the Union ironclad *Monitor* in battle. Neither ship won the battle, but the *Monitor* very nearly destroyed the fearsome Confederate ship.

Late in April came more concrete news. Lincoln received word that flag officer David Farragut had led his ships into the mouth of the Mississippi and captured the Southern stronghold of New Orleans. Also, by May, General McClellan had finally begun to move. He marched through Virginia and forced the Confederate army to abandon the city of Norfolk.

Later in the month, Union troops captured Pensacola, Florida, and Baton Rouge, Louisiana. The South's important harbor towns were now in Union hands. The slow blockade that wise old General Scott had talked about at the beginning of the war could now begin to take effect.

Although General McClellan had overtaken Norfolk, Virginia, Lincoln was still not pleased with him. McClellan had his own agenda for carrying out the war, and he followed the president's orders only when he had to. Trying to keep control of his general, Lincoln asked for frequent reports detailing specific information. McClellan bristled. To show that he thought the order was pointless, he sent the president a mocking telegraph that ran: "We have just captured six cows. What shall we do with them?"

Lincoln read the telegraph, smiled, and sent a reply: "As to the six cows captured—milk them."

But despite the few moments of humor, President Lincoln worried about his general. In June, McClellan met up with the commander-in-chief of the Confederate forces, Robert E. Lee, at Mechanicsville, Virginia. Over the next seven days, the two armies flew repeatedly at each other. Corpses piled high as the fighting in the Civil War reached new heights of horror. In those seven days, more than 30,000 Union and Confederate soldiers were killed. Neither side won a smashing victory, but McClellan was the one forced into retreat. Yet McClellan's army was greater than Lee's by 15,000 men.

The North was shocked by the scale of bloodshed and by the defeat. President Lincoln was especially stunned by the loss of life. Senator Orville Browning visited him in his White House office. "He looked weary, care-worn and troubled," Browning wrote. "I shook hands with him, and asked him how he was. He said 'tolerably well.' I remarked that I felt concerned about him— regretted that troubles crowded so heavily upon him, and feared his health was suffering. He held me by the hand, pressed it, and said in a very tender and touching tone—'Browning, I must die sometime.'"

Senator Browning was worried at how depressed the president had become. He told Lincoln: "... your fortunes Mr. President are bound up with those of the Country... and I hope you will do all you can to preserve your health and life."

Lincoln was pained by the mounting violence of the war. He was also furious with McClellan. Still, he gave his general one more chance. On September 17, McClellan and Lee again met near Sharpsburg, Virginia, this time at Antietam Creek. Lee's men were well entrenched. McClellan led his men on one attack after another. Corpses littered the ground by the day's end. The next night, Lee retreated. For some unknown reason, McClellan did not pursue. The Battle of Antietam was the bloodiest one-day battle of the war. At its end, 12,000 Union soldiers and almost 9,000 Confederates lay dead. Lee had given way, and McClellan had won an important victory.

But in Washington, Lincoln and his advisors were angry and confused. Why had McClellan let the wily Lee escape? Lincoln was fed up with McClellan's cautious approach and removed him from command. Over the next several months the president tried out a series of generals, each of whom was not quite right to lead the army.

First he chose Major General Henry Halleck to lead the armies. Halleck had won significant victories in Missouri and Tennessee. Now he came east to try to succeed where McClellan had failed. But Halleck, a stiff, formal man, did not work out either.

Lincoln met with McClellan at Antietam Creek and urged the general to attack Lee.

McClellan—still in charge of an army in Virginia—quarreled with him. Halleck, McClellan, and John Pope, another general Lincoln counted on, could not seem to coordinate their armies.

Robert E. Lee, opposing the superior Union forces in the mountains of Virginia, made use of their situation. He and Stonewall Jackson outwitted and crushed the Union armies in successive battles during late August of 1862.

Lincoln was at his wits' end. Where could he find a man with the energy, daring, and intellect of Lee? His next move was to put Ambrose Burnside in charge of the Army of the Potomac. Burnside was an eager general, but did not prove to be a natural leader. In December he faced off against the combined armies of Lee and Jackson in Fredericksburg, Virginia. He was forced into retreat. Once again, Lincoln was at a loss for leadership.

While the fighting wore on and Abraham Lincoln continued to hope for a general who could lead the North to victory, he had developed another plan. In late July 1862 he had assembled his cabinet and read a remarkable document to them. He called it the Emancipation Proclamation. In it, he proposed to free all the slaves in the seceded states.

Lincoln's position had always been that slavery must come to an end. He was considered to be moderate at the time on the question of slavery. More extreme were the abolitionists, who had been crying out for an immediate end to slavery. Lincoln had never disagreed with them that slavery was wrong. He had simply believed that the South, and many people in the North, would not go along with total emancipation, or freedom. The South had too much money staked in its slaves.

But now, as president of a country that was at war with itself, Lincoln must have felt that the time was right for a drastic move. After all, the South had already broken away. The only tricky question involved the border states of Kentucky, Maryland, and Missouri. Slavery was still legal in these states, yet they remained loyal to the Union. Lincoln did not want to drive them to the Confederacy. That was why his Emancipation Proclamation proposed to free all slaves only in the rebellious states.

He had tried one other tactic, but that had failed. In March 1862, he had proposed to Congress a bill that would have offered *all* states payment in exchange for freeing their slaves, to help make up for the loss of their "property." Lincoln thought some of the Southern states might have found this a good way to end the war. But none were interested. Therefore, he made a bold decision. He would

This painting shows Lincoln with his cabinet as he signed the Emancipation Proclamation.

declare complete, total, uncompensated freedom for all slaves in Rebel states.

In September, Lincoln made the Proclamation public. It was to go into effect on January 1, 1863. On that date, the nearly 4 million slaves in the Confederacy would be technically free. Of course, the Confederate government had other ideas.

GETTYSBURG

"...we cannot dedicate, we cannot consecrate, we
cannot hallow, this ground. The brave men,
living and dead, who struggled here, have
consecrated it, far above our power to add or to
detract."

ABRAHAM LINCOLN,
THE GETTYSBURG ADDRESS

The summer of 1863 marked the turning point of the Civil
War. Two great battles crushed the hopes of the Confederate States of America for independence. One battle
was fought to the west, on the Mississippi River. The other took
place in the east, amid the rolling hills of Pennsylvania.

Robert E. Lee must have felt as though the whole weight of the
Confederacy was on his back. The war had been turning slowly
and steadily in favor of the North. A great blow would have to be
struck if the South were to turn the tide. Lee brought his Army of
Northern Virginia across the Potomac. His objective was to invade
the North. If he could win a series of victories in Northern
territory, perhaps the course of the war would change.

Lee marched his men hard. In the heat of June, with his army
stretched out along 60 miles, he got word that the great Army of
the Potomac was approaching him. Lee had to get his scattered
troops together. Looking at the map, he put his finger on the tiny
town of Gettysburg, Pennsylvania. He would meet up with the
enemy there.

On July 1, all of Lee's men had gathered. Lee faced a new opponent. Lincoln had given command of the army of the Potomac to General George Meade, a tough, gruff veteran who had commanded a division under McClellan at Antietam. Meade and the bulk of his army had not yet reached Gettysburg when John Buford, commander of Meade's cavalry regiment, collided with Lee. Buford's men had taken to high ground, a place called Seminary Ridge. There they battled valiantly throughout the morning. But the Confederate army was too vast. At day's end, Buford's men were either dead or had scattered.

By the next morning, most of Meade's army had arrived and the real battle began. Again the Union army had the high ground: a peak called Cemetery Hill and a long ridge that extended south from it. The Confederates charged in separate units, trying to punch holes in Meade's flanks. Artillery boomed and rifles cracked. Cries of agony filled the air. Lee's men fought bravely for their beloved commander. It was one of the rare battles in which the Confederate troops were the attackers and the Union soldiers held a defensive line.

At the end of the day the hillsides were strewn with corpses, both in gray and blue. The wailing of the wounded went on all night, while the generals of each side met and tried to guess what the morning would bring. The nauseating smell of rotting corpses wafted over the battlefield as men on both sides squeezed their eyes shut and tried not to think of the next day.

The morning of July 3 was hot and windless. It began with a bang as Lee directed a wicked charge at the right flank of Meade's line of defense. The soldiers entrenched there fought the Rebels back, then everyone waited to see what Lee's next move would be. It came a few hours later: a great, echoing, piercing artillery blast. All along the Confederate lines, the cannons blasted away, kicking back with each firing. The barrels grew hot enough to fry bacon on, but still Lee continued the attack. Shells rained in on the Army of the Potomac, but Meade's men held their position. They answered the fire and waited.

At last, Lee called off the fire. In mid-afternoon he was ready to make his final play. Fifteen thousand infantry soldiers carefully moved into neat columns, banners flapping and rifles ready. Confederate General George Pickett raised his sword. It flashed in the bright sun. "Charge!" he cried. And 15,000 men marched up the hill in one final, brave attempt to break the enemy line.

This was one of the bloodiest moments of the Civil War. The hearty cries of the charging soldiers, the blast of gunfire, and the screams of the wounded and dying created a din that the survivors remembered all their lives. Forty years later, as the 20th century was drawing near, old men who had fought at Gettysburg still told the terrible tale of Pickett's Charge.

In the end, Pickett's line was destroyed. The Union troops held Cemetery Ridge. The Battle of Gettysburg was over and more than 40,000 men lay dead. Robert E. Lee's valiant invasion of the North had failed.

The victory was an important one for the North, but also a costly one. More than 20,000 Union soldiers had lost their lives at Gettysburg. And, though Meade had stopped Lee's invasion

More than 40,000 men lost their lives on the fields of Gettysburg.

hopes, Lee's army was still intact. Just as McClellan had failed to pursue Lee after Antietam, Meade did not follow the retreating army after Gettysburg.

Gettysburg quickly became known as the one battle that best represented the Civil War. It was the clash of the two great armies of the North and the South: the Army of the Potomac and the Army of Northern Virginia. Shortly after the battle, with the war still raging in other areas, people decided that a ceremony ought to be held at Gettysburg to commemorate the battle and the men who had lost their lives fighting for their beliefs.

The ceremony took place on November 19, 1863. A crowd estimated at 20,000 people filled the field where the battle had taken place four months before. In it were congressmen, governors, business tycoons, civic groups, and thousands of ordinary farm families. They were all there to hear the speech of Edward Everett, the most famous orator of the day, who had been asked to honor the battle with a few unforgettable words.

Everett spoke for two hours. The crowd listened politely as he recounted the battle and talked of the importance of the great war they were still in the midst of. It was a fine speech, filled with the dignified, flowery phrases popular at the time.

Near the end of the program came the time for the president of the United States to make a few remarks. Lincoln had ridden the train here especially to honor the battle. He was not to be the main speaker, so he had not prepared a speech before he left. Instead, he waited until he was on the train. He sat listening to his advisors chatter about the upcoming event, then excused himself, saying, "Gentlemen, this is all very pleasant, but the people will expect me to say something to them tomorrow, and I must give the matter some thought."

Lincoln sat by himself on the train, did some thinking, and scribbled out a few sentences. He wanted to say that the Civil War was a test of the principles of the founding fathers, who had begun the United States as a great experiment in democracy. He wanted to keep his speech short, since he was not the main speaker. When he

This rare photo captured the scene at the Gettysburg battlefield commemoration.

addressed the crowd at Gettysburg, he talked for only three minutes. He said:

> Fourscore and seven years ago, our fathers brought forth upon this continent a new nation, conceived in liberty and dedicated to the proposition that all men are created equal.
>
> Now we are engaged in a great civil war, testing whether that nation—or any nation, so conceived and so dedicated—can long endure.
>
> We are met on a great battlefield of that war. We are met to dedicate a portion of it as the final resting place of those who have given their lives that that nation might live.
>
> It is altogether fitting and proper that we should do this.
>
> But, in a larger sense, we cannot dedicate, we cannot consecrate, we cannot hallow, this ground. The brave men, living and dead, who struggled here, have consecrated it, far above our power to add or to detract.
>
> The world will very little note nor long remember what we say here, but it can never forget what they did here.
>
> It is for us, the living, rather, to be dedicated, here, to the unfinished work that they have thus far so nobly carried on. It is rather for us to be here dedicated to the great task remaining before us; that from these honored dead we take increased devotion to that

cause for which they here gave the last full measure of devotion; that we here highly resolve that these dead shall not have died in vain; that the nation shall, under God, have a new birth of freedom, and that the government of the people by the people, and for the people, shall not perish from the earth.

Lincoln's words were not considered greatly moving by most people at the time they were delivered. The crowd clapped politely. Newspapers simply noted that "the dedicatory remarks were then delivered by the President."

But in time his words grew in importance. They came to stand as the greatest statement of what the Civil War was about. Unlike Everett's long speech, Lincoln's remarks were brief and to the point. They were simple enough for children to understand. Lincoln said, "The world will very little note nor long remember what we say here, but it can never forget what they did here." In fact, it is largely because of Lincoln's Gettysburg Address that people still remember the historic battle and what it meant.

A GENERAL AND A VICTORY

"With malice toward none, with charity for all . . ."

ABRAHAM LINCOLN'S SECOND
INAUGURAL ADDRESS

While Robert E. Lee's Army of Northern Virginia and George Meade's Army of the Potomac were flying at one another across the fields of Gettysburg, another major contest was being decided in the West. The Mississippi River was one of the important prizes of the war. The Confederacy controlled much of it south of Kentucky, and Lincoln was determined to take it from them. His chief of operations in the West was a gruff, whiskey-drinking man named Ulysses S. Grant. Grant was only 40 years old, but he had proven himself a fine military man in his two years of duty in the West.

In November 1862, Grant began a campaign to capture the important river city of Vicksburg, Mississippi. This proved to be an enormously difficult task. Grant had to maneuver a huge army across hundreds of miles of unfamiliar territory, battle the considerable western armies of the South, and open up the Mississippi River.

Nevertheless, he set to his task with great energy. In February, Lincoln and his men in Washington got word that Grant had opened part of the river so that Union gunboats could get through.

In April, the boats, under the command of David Dixon Porter, forced their way past the Vicksburg forts. Next came word that Grant had won an important victory at Port Gibson, Mississippi, just south of Vicksburg. In May, the brash young general won a series of astounding victories around Vicksburg. He was circling in for the kill.

But Vicksburg itself proved too tough to defeat by attack. Grant's guns pounded away, but the city held. Therefore, at the end of May, Grant had his men dig a line of trenches 17 miles long around the city. They would lay siege until the Confederates were forced to give up.

The Southern troops in Vicksburg held on for nearly six weeks. Then, on July 3, the same day that Lee lost the Battle of Gettysburg, the Rebel troops surrendered. Vicksburg was in Union hands. The Confederates could no longer use the mighty Mississippi River for supplies and communication. It was the beginning of the end of the war.

In Washington, cheers went up. Lincoln asked for information about General Grant. His aides reported that Grant was an able man, but that he had several problems. Lincoln was curious. What kind of problems? Grant tended to be rude, the aides reported, and he was known throughout the army for his carelessness. He was a sloppy dresser. Abraham Lincoln was not known for being a smooth talker or an elegant dresser himself. He was not about to hold such things against a man. But the aides had more to say. Grant's biggest problem, they reported, was that he was a heavy drinker.

According to some, Lincoln smiled when he heard this, and roared: "Find out what he drinks and send a barrel of it to my other generals!"

On January 1, 1863, the Emancipation Proclamation formally went into effect. All Southern blacks were now technically free. But the Confederacy had not given up yet. They would fight on to keep their traditions. Robert E. Lee was gearing up for battle again in Virginia.

Grant distinguished himself as a brigadier general in the western theater.

Lincoln now made a momentous decision. He called Ulysses S. Grant to Washington and formally appointed him commander-in-chief of all Union armies. Here, Lincoln believed, was a man with unrelenting drive, with courage, and with daring. McClellan had been too cautious. Halleck lacked the respect of the troops. Meade had not taken advantage of his superiority. But Grant had none of these faults. The Union army needed to make one grand push to bring the Confederacy to its knees. He was the man for the job.

On June 7, 1864, the Republican Convention, meeting in Baltimore, renominated Abraham Lincoln as their party's candidate for president. Andrew Johnson of Tennessee was selected as his vice presidential running mate.

The Democrats nominated none other than General George B. McClellan. No longer in command, McClellan was still arguing with Lincoln's handling of the war. He and his fellow Democrats were calling for an immediate end to the war. The Republicans argued that this would make the deaths of all the brave soldiers who had given their lives for their country meaningless.

Most of the country agreed with the Republicans. Still, if the war was going to drag on much longer, many people were in favor of ending it now. After the victories of Gettysburg and Vicksburg, there came a long uncertain period. General Grant was now skirmishing with Robert E. Lee's army in Virginia, and he was proving to be a match for the great Virginian. No major victory had been won yet, but Grant was steadily wearing down the Confederate army.

The country was eager for big news, however. Lincoln needed it if he was to be reelected.

Then, away to the South, Admiral Farragut delivered some news. He had blasted his way into Mobile Bay, closing off the final Southern port on the Gulf of Mexico. A month later, General William Sherman captured the city of Atlanta. With these two victories, the people of the North relaxed. The end of the war was near.

On November 8, they elected Abraham Lincoln to a second term as president by a huge margin. Lincoln won by more than

400,000 votes, the biggest margin any president had been reelected by until that time. (Of course, citizens of the Confederacy did not vote.)

Once more, on March 4, 1865, Lincoln stood outside the Capitol and took the oath of office. This time the brand new Capitol dome was in place. Lincoln had aged a great deal during his four years as president. The lines in his face were deeper; his eyes were sad and tired. He was 56 years old, but he looked older.

As the war had progressed, Mary noticed a sadness creeping into her husband's soul. His legendary joke-telling trickled off. He ate little. For lunch he might have only a biscuit, an apple, and a glass

The photo at left was taken in 1861, just after Lincoln's election. Just four years later, the president seemed to have aged a lifetime (right).

of milk. He had grown painfully thin, about 35 pounds underweight for a man his size. His doctors feared he would soon suffer a breakdown due to exhaustion. In the previous four years, Abraham Lincoln had seen more suffering than he ever thought possible. But he now had good reason to believe it was coming to an end.

This time the inaugural oath was given by Salmon Chase, the old rival whom Lincoln had appointed secretary of the treasury. More recently, he had appointed Chase chief justice of the Supreme Court.

In his second inaugural address, Lincoln spoke with wisdom and compassion, calling for the country to finish the task:

> With malice toward none, with charity for all, with firmness in the right as God gives us to see the right, let us strive on to finish the work we are in, to bind up the nation's wounds, to care for him who shall have borne the battle and for his widow and his orphan, to do all which may achieve and cherish a just and a lasting peace among ourselves and with all nations.

One month later, the president received a cable from Union forces in the Confederate capital. It said simply, "We took Richmond at 8:15 this morning." The Confederate government had fled the day before. The city was in Union hands.

The people of the North were joyous. Headlines cried: "Richmond Is Ours!" In Washington, New York, Baltimore, Detroit, and many other cities people ran into the streets cheering. Schools were let out. Young girls danced. Old women wept.

The president took the news quietly. He decided that he wanted to see the city for himself. His cabinet officers advised against it, fearing an assassination attempt. But Lincoln went anyway. He arrived on a steamer the next day. Accompanied by a military escort, he walked through the streets while stunned Southerners watched in silence from their windows.

A group of blacks realized who the tall stranger was and ran up to him crying for joy. Some knelt at his feet and tried to kiss his shoes. Lincoln was horrified. "This is not right," he said. "You must kneel to God only, and thank him for the liberty you will hereafter enjoy."

Then the president entered the Executive Mansion at which the Confederate government had met just the day before. The building looked old and rundown. President Lincoln sat in Jefferson Davis's own chair, looking as old and shopworn as the building. Then he left.

One week later, General Robert E. Lee finally realized his cause was hopeless. Grant had steadily strangled his supply lines and worn his shrinking army to the bone. Lee gathered his remaining men and limped toward the small town of Appomattox Courthouse, Virginia.

There, on April 9, 1865, Lee and Grant met face to face. They talked about the Mexican War, which both men had served in. They had many things in common. Then Grant offered his terms for surrender. Lee accepted them, asking only that his men be allowed to keep their horses, for most were farmers who would need them. Grant agreed. Then Lee surrendered the Army of Northern Virginia to Grant. The South still had armies fighting a bit longer in the South and West, but the leaders had surrendered. The Civil War was over.

Richmond was a scene of desolation as President Lincoln took his tour of the city.

THE FINAL ACT

"O Captain! my Captain! our fearful trip is
    done..."

WALT WHITMAN

Five days after the Civil War ended, Mary Todd Lincoln asked her husband to take her to the theater. She knew he always loved plays. He kept a complete set of Shakespeare's works in his White House office. But Abe Lincoln did not feel like going. He was tired. Besides, the play, *Our American Cousin,* was supposed to be a silly farce. He preferred something with more substance to it.

But Mrs. Lincoln persisted, so in the end he agreed to go. What's more, General Grant was in town, and Mrs. Lincoln wanted him to accompany them. She thought the citizens of Washington would like to get a look at their war hero.

Washington was still in the midst of celebrations. Cannons fired periodically in the city squares. The streets were still littered from the victory parade that had been held three days before.

The parade had ended at the White House, where the huge throng of people gathered to hear the president speak. They were wildly enthusiastic, eager to show their love for the man who had steered the nation through the Civil War. They wanted to hear a stirring, emotional speech. But Lincoln did not give it to them. Instead, he used the occasion to put before the people his plan for healing the nation.

The crowd wanted to hear him say he would punish the South and hang its leaders. But Lincoln talked of the future, and of the need for the North and South to work as one nation again. He outlined plans for rebuilding the battered Southern states. And then, most shocking of all, he said that he wanted to give the newly freed blacks the right to vote.

The crowd clapped politely, but there was more confusion than pleasure on their faces.

Now, three days later, Lincoln spent the early afternoon further outlining his plans for reconstructing the South and healing the nation. He met with various cabinet officers and with General Grant. "We must reanimate the states [get them moving again]," he told them.

A big question was what they should do with the leaders of the Confederacy. Many congressmen were in favor of putting them to death. Lincoln preferred a more gentle approach. "I hope that there will be no persecution," he said, "no bloody work after the war is over. No one need expect me to take any part in hanging or killing these men, even the worst of them." Lincoln said he would be happy if the Confederate leaders escaped from the country. Then the government would not be forced to take measures against them.

It was Good Friday—the day Christians believe that Jesus was killed—so many people had the day off from work. But President Lincoln worked on. He would have his bit of diversion in the evening.

Stanton, his bulldog-like secretary of war, begged the president not to go to the theater, as he had done many times before. Stanton was always worried about assassination plots. He had spent much of his time during the last few years sending spies out to uncover such plots. Stanton's constant fear now was that the Confederate government would make one last desperate attempt to turn the situation around by killing the president.

Long ago, Lincoln had given in to Stanton and accepted an around-the-clock bodyguard. In his customary way, Lincoln had befriended the men assigned to guard him, and he had often sat swapping stories with them. Now Lincoln said that although he did not really want to go to the theater, he would to go please his wife. And he would take a guard with him.

At 8:25, the president's carriage arrived at Ford's Theater, several blocks east of the White House. General Grant, who was always very uncomfortable among high society, had politely declined the offer to accompany the president and his wife. Instead, a young friend of Mary's, Clara Harris, and her fiancé, Major Henry Rathbone, joined them.

The play was already in progress. When President Lincoln himself led his party into the theater, the play stopped and everyone in the theater applauded. Ford's was packed that night, for the theater had advertised the president's appearance in a quickly printed handbill that was distributed all over town:

THIS EVENING THE PERFORMANCE WILL BE HONORED BY THE PRESENCE OF PRESIDENT LINCOLN

This was just the sort of thing that made Secretary of War Stanton cringe. Lincoln always liked appearing in public. He was aware of the possibility of assassination. He often said, "If they kill me, the next man will be just as bad for them. In a country like this, where our habits are simple, and must be, assassination is always possible, and will come if they are determined upon it."

Still, just a few days earlier the president had startled his wife by telling her of a dream he had had in which he walked downstairs in the White House to a room in which a body lay covered. He asked the attendant who had died, and the man said, "The President. He was killed by an assassin." This upset Mary, and Abe said, "It is only a dream, Mary. Let us say no more about it, and try to forget it."

The president's party walked up to their private box. They took their seats, and the play resumed. The guard was stationed just outside the door to the box.

Abe Lincoln may have become interested in the play, or he may have been thinking about all he had accomplished, or what he wanted to accomplish. People later said that he had been unusually happy that day. It would make sense. After all, the man who had been raised in the backwoods of Kentucky, Indiana, and Illinois, who had worked as a shopkeeper, a postmaster, and a surveyer, who said "cheer" for "chair" and "git" for "get," had done well for himself.

No one would have expected a "country lawyer" to have the ability and intelligence to lead the country through its most stormy years. Lincoln had done it, however. The nation would stay in one piece. Now the people respected him, looked upon him as a father figure, and hoped he would lead them in healing the war wounds.

Shortly after 10 o'clock, a hand aimed a pistol at the back of the president's head. Just as the actor on stage delivered a funny line, the gun went off. The sound was muffled by the audience's laughter. The bullet entered Lincoln's neck and lodged in his brain. His head slumped forward.

The man who had fired the gun was a young actor named John Wilkes Booth. He was well-known and came from a family of Shakespearean actors. In fact, had President Lincoln gotten a look at the man, he might have recognized the handsome young face. But Lincoln never knew he was there.

Major Rathbone turned and saw the young man. He did not know what had happened, but he knew this man had no reason to be in the box. As it turned out, the guard had left his post to get a view of the play. Rathbone lunged for the man, but Booth had a knife in his other hand. He slashed the major with it and flung himself over the railing onto the stage. His leg caught in the flag that hung down from the box, and in his awkward fall he broke his left leg. He limped across the stage, still clutching the bloody knife, and was gone.

The hall erupted in panic. A doctor made his way to the box and began checking the president for signs of life. Mrs. Lincoln was wild-eyed with terror, unable to believe what had happened. Word spread into the streets, and soon a huge crowd had gathered in front of the theater. Other doctors arrived. They determined that the president still lived, but they could see it was hopeless.

Booth shot Lincoln from the right side of the president's box at Ford's Theater.

Soldiers cleared a path through the growing throng, and Lincoln was carried out into the street. Across the street a man named Petersen was motioning from his porch. They brought the president into his house and laid him on a bed. The bed was too small for his lanky body, so he was laid diagonally across it, with his feet dangling off.

Meanwhile, across town, Secretary of State William Seward was attacked by a man with a knife at almost the same instant. Seward's son, daughter, and an attendant were also wounded as the man escaped.

Soon rumors were flying across the city of a Confederate plot to assassinate the entire federal government. Secretary of War Stanton, who had always feared such a plot, arrived at the Petersen house. The vice president was alerted. Stanton ordered guards for every White House official. Many in the audience named the actor John Wilkes Booth as the killer. Stanton assumed Ford's Theater had been in on the plot and ordered every employee arrested. He set about thinking how best to cope with what he thought was a major plot against the government.

In fact, as far as anyone can tell today, the plot did not involve the Confederate leaders. It was Booth and a few of his friends, all staunch Southern loyalists, who had hatched the scheme. Booth saw it as a last-ditch way to save the day for the Confederate States of America. As it turned out, he had shot one of the few men in the federal government who favored treating the Southern states gently.

Booth was able to escape into Maryland. Twelve days later Federal troops caught up with him on a farm in Virginia. He was shot during the chase, or some say he may have shot himself. He died a short time later.

All night people waited in front of the Petersen house. Inside, the doctors kept a steady watch over the president. Mary Lincoln sat in the next room in stunned silence. Occasionally she would cry out. "Why did he not shoot me instead of my husband?" she wailed. Robert, her eldest son, arrived from the White House. He looked at his father. A great purple patch was spreading around the right eye. He sat beside his mother and held her hands.

The cabinet members and senators who gathered in the room throughout the long night each took their turn staring down at the gaunt face. Lincoln had led them all through the turbulence. They had all differed with him many times. Yet all of them had come to depend on his calm, strong leadership, his humor, and his deep love of humanity.

Soon newspapers would be printing their black-bordered eulogies of the remarkable man who came out of the West at just the right moment to steer his nation through its darkest days. They would note how strange it was that this tragedy had occurred within days of the end of the war. They would call him "the man for the hour."

Soon whole cities that now celebrated the end of war would be filled with grief. All business would stop. Flags would fly at half mast. Strangers would meet in the street, begin discussing the terrible news, and burst into tears.

Many of the great men who assembled in Petersen's house wondered how the nation would heal itself without Lincoln to lead the way. It would be up to them.

At 7:22 the next morning, Abraham Lincoln stopped breathing. The doctors quietly noted the time of death. Mary Lincoln was brought into the room. "Oh my God!" she moaned. "I have given my husband to die!" Her son led her away.

Edwin Stanton looked tenderly at the body and said simply, "Now he belongs to the ages."

EPILOGUE

Soon after John Wilkes Booth shot his bullet, Abraham Lincoln became a figure of legend. Tales of his wisdom and wit spread far and wide. During the war there had been a great deal of criticism of Lincoln from newspapers, politicians, and ordinary citizens. Some thought he was weak; others thought he took on the powers of a king or tyrant, such as when he suspended the writ of habeas corpus. After the assassination, all such criticism stopped. Abraham Lincoln had brought the Civil War to an end. He had saved the nation and lost his life. Nothing else mattered.

As the decades went on, Lincoln was transformed into myth. Other, much older nations had mythical figures from their past. Greece had the wise philosopher Socrates. Italy had Renaissance artists like Michelangelo and Leonardo da Vinci. England had Shakespeare. The United States had its founding fathers, who had created the first working democracy in the modern world. And now it had Abraham Lincoln, who saw the nation through its darkest days.

More books have been written about Lincoln than about all of the other presidents put together. That is partly because the Civil War was a unique moment in American history and Lincoln came to power at just the right time to preserve the Union. It is also because many people feel that Abraham Lincoln represents the American ideal: a man of humble beginnings who rose to greatness.

ABRAHAM LINCOLN

Feb. 12, 1809	Born in a log cabin near Hodgenville, Kentucky
1816	Family moves to southwest Indiana
1818	Nancy Hanks Lincoln, Abe's mother, dies
1830	The Lincolns move to Illinois
1831	Abe moves to New Salem, Illinois
1832	Abe becomes a captain in the Black Hawk War
1834	Elected to Illinois state legislature
1836	Begins law practice
1842	Marries Mary Todd
1847–49	Serves in the U.S. House of Representatives
1858	Lincoln and Douglas hold a series of debates across Illinois as they contest Douglas's Senate seat Lincoln becomes known nationwide as a Republican spokesman
1860	Lincoln is nominated Republican candidate for president Lincoln is elected president South Carolina secedes from the Union
1861	Lincoln is inaugurated as the sixteenth president of the Union Fort Sumter falls
1862	Lincoln calls for 300,000 men to enlist for three years
1863	Lincoln issues the Emancipation Proclamation
1864	Lincoln re-elected; Andrew Johnson is elected vice president
1865	The Confederate capital of Richmond falls Lincoln visits Richmond Lee surrenders to Grant at Appomattox Courthouse John Wilkes Booth shoots Lincoln in Washington, D.C.
April 15, 1865	Lincoln dies

Suggested Reading

Catton, Bruce. *The Civil War*. New York: Houghton Mifflin, 1987 (originally published 1960).

*Coffey, Vincent. *The Battle of Gettysburg*. Morristown, N.J.: Silver Burdett, 1985.

*Foster, Genevieve. *1861: Year of Lincoln*. New York: Scribners, 1970.

Freedman, Russell. *Lincoln: A Photobiography*. New York: Clarion Press, 1987.

Jennison, Keith W. *The Humorous Mr. Lincoln*. Woodstock, Vt.: Country Press, 1965.

Kolpas, Norman. *Abraham Lincoln*. New York: McGraw-Hill, 1981.

Latham, Frank B. *Lincoln and the Emancipation Proclamation*. New York: Franklin Watts, 1969.

Russell, Sharman Apt. *Frederick Douglass*. New York: Chelsea House, 1988.

Sandburg, Carl. *Abe Lincoln Grows Up*. New York: Harcourt, Brace, 1926.

*Sterling, Dorothy. *Forever Free: The Story of the Emancipation Proclamation*. New York: Doubleday, 1963.

*Readers of *Abraham Lincoln: To Preserve the Union* will find these books particularly readable.

Selected Sources

CIVIL WAR

Catton, Bruce. *This Hallowed Ground*. New York: Washington Square Press, 1961 (originally published 1955).

Catton, Bruce. *The Civil War.* New York: Houghton Mifflin 1987 (originally published 1960).

Commager, Henry Steele, ed. *The Blue and the Gray.* Indianapolis: Bobbs-Merrill, 1950.

Johnson, Robert Underwood, and Clarence Clough Buel, eds. *Battles and Leaders of the Civil War.* 4 vols. New York: 1884–87.

McPherson, James. *Battle Cry of Freedom.* New York: Oxford University Press, 1988.

Pressly, Thomas J. *Americans Interpret Their Civil War.* New York: The Free Press, 1962.

Schlesinger, Arthur M., Jr. *The Age of Jackson.* Boston: Little, Brown, 1953.

United States War Department. *War of the Rebellion: a Compilation of the Official Records of the Union and Confederate Armies,* 1902.

Wiltse, Charles. *The New Nation: 1800–1845.* New York: Hill and Wang, 1961.

LINCOLN

Angle, Paul ed. *Created Equal?: The Complete Lincoln-Douglas Debates of 1858.* Chicago: University of Chicago, 1958.

Baker, Jean. *Mary Todd Lincoln.* New York: W. W. Norton, 1987.

Boritt, G. S. *Lincoln and the Economics of the American Dream.* Memphis, TN: Memphis State University Press, 1978.

Carpenter, F. B. *Six Months at the White House with Abraham Lincoln.* New York: Hurd & Houghton, 1867.

Chase, Salmon P. *Inside Lincoln's Cabinet: The Civil War Diaries of Salmon P. Chase.* New York: Longman, Green and Co., 1954.

Cox, LaWanda. *Lincoln and Black Freedom.* Columbia: University of South Carolina Press, 1981.

Davis, Michael. *The Image of Lincoln in the South.* Knoxville: University of Tennessee Press, 1971.

Dennett, Tyler, ed. *Lincoln and the Civil War in the Diaries and Letters of John Hay.* New York: Dodd, Mead & Co., 1939.

Herndon, William H. and Jesse W. Weik. *Herndon's Life of Lincoln*. Cleveland: World Publishing Co., 1942 (reissued by Da Capo Press, 1983).

Mitgang, Herbert, ed. *Abraham Lincoln: A Press Portrait*. Chicago: Quadrangle Books, 1971.

Nicolay, John and John Hay. *Abraham Lincoln: A History*. 10 vols. New York: The Century Co., 1890.

Oates, Stephen B. *With Malice Toward None: The Life of Abraham Lincoln*. New York: Harper & Row, 1977.

Rice, A. T., ed. *Reminiscences of Abraham Lincoln by Distinguished Men of His Time*, 1886.

Sandburg, Carl. *Abraham Lincoln: The Prairie Years and The War Years in One Volume*. New York: Harcourt Brace Jovanovich, 1954.

Stephenson, N. W. *An Autobiography of Abraham Lincoln*. Indianapolis: Bobbs Merrill 1926.

Thomas, Benjamin. *Abraham Lincoln*. New York: Alfred A. Knopf, 1952.

Williams, T. Harry. *Lincoln and the Radicals*. Madison: University of Wisconsin Press, 1965.

Index

Russell Shorto was born in Johnstown, Pennsylvania. He has written ten books for children, including biographies of Thomas Jefferson, Edgar Allan Poe, J.R.R. Tolkien, and the American Indian leaders Tecumseh and Geronimo. He has also written for such magazines as *Gentlemen's Quarterly* and *Travel & Leisure*. He lives in New York City.